The Spoiled Brat Killer

Larry Maravich

Published by Trellis Publishing, 2021.

While every precaution has been taken in the preparation of this book, the publisher assumes no responsibility for errors or omissions, or for damages resulting from the use of the information contained herein.

THE SPOILED BRAT KILLER

First edition. July 9, 2021.

Copyright © 2021 Larry Maravich.

ISBN: 979-8224919796

Written by Larry Maravich.

THE SPOILED BRAT KILLER

LARRY MARAVICH

Taylor Marks – The Girl For Whom It All Went Wrong

Taylor Marks appeared to be young lady with everything going for her. Financial security, a loving mother prepared, it seemed, to do anything for a much-loved daughter. Why then, would she pay a friend $5000 to kill that caring parent?

Like so much in life, Taylor Marks' story is much more complicated than appears on the surface. Today, as she sits in an Ohio prison, knowing that she will die without ever again being free, we can wonder about her thoughts. To what extent does she regret her actions? And what is the full degree of her guilt?

Her parents, Kristie and Bruce Marks were a couple unable to have children of their own. They adopted Taylor when she was a young child, never hiding the fact that they were not her biological parents. Not that this seemed to be any kind of problem. Friends report that Taylor was never concerned about her history, and never seemed to demonstrate any interest in finding her biological parents. For Bruce and Kristie, they poured everything they had into their daughter, lavishing her with her gifts and love. Her friend, Lauren Smith, told of how the young girl have 'everything she needed, and more.'

Bonnie Monteleone, a close family friend of the Marks, says that both Bruce and Kristie gave their daughter everything she wanted. While, according to Bonnie, Kristie always demanded some responsibility in return for the outlay poured onto their child, for Bruce, it was just a question of outright spoiling, a daddy giving everything to his gorgeous girl.

The Marks lived in New Jersey, close to the base of Bruce's telecommunications business. There was much travel, visiting all corners of the US, as that business took the managing director far and wide. Often, Kristie and Taylor would go along for the ride, impromptu breaks that tied the family even closer together.

Taylor was incredibly devoted to her father, a real daddy's girl. Then, suddenly, when she was just thirteen years old – an incredibly vulnerable age – Bruce died. There was no warning, no chance to prepare for this. One moment he was there, the next, he had gone.

Both Taylor and her mother were devastated. Taylor was close to moving to her High School, and entering those difficult teenage years. With Bruce's business providing for the whole family in relative comfort, Kristie had been a stay at home mum. She realised that, although there was money around – plenty of it – it would not last forever.

She decided that she would need to find a job. But to help cope with this, her growing daughter and the loss of her husband and the family breadwinner, it made sense to move across the country and back to Ohio, where her family lived.

The family moved just in time for Taylor to join her High School. Akron, in North East Ohio is a relatively disadvantaged city in an impoverished part of the state. However, Copley High School served the children of the wealthy who lived in the most comfortably off part of the town. It was a school with a good reputation, teaching largely interested students whose parents were supportive of education, and wanted the best academic outcomes for their children.

Yet it appears as though Copley High School did little for this keen but grieving girl. She had travelled across the nation to enter an institution where she knew almost nobody to any real extent. What the school did discover, relatively quickly, was that Taylor had some kind of academic problems, Bonnie Monteleone describing it as probably a specific learning difficulty.

Whatever it was, the bright little girl started to struggle with her work. She found it increasingly difficult to cope, and began to lose interest in her education. Taylor began to mix with undesirable types, and as she grew older, a reputation she would have preferred to avoid began to attach itself to her.

As well as struggling academically, and still desperately missing her father, she was an immature girl, and started to gather a number of boyfriends, relations with whom did not last long. She garnered a reputation as an 'easy lay' even being called a 'whore' at times.

Within three or four years of her father's death, the girl who seemed to have everything going for her had become a failure at school, developed an unsavoury reputation, and was growing rebellious towards her mother.

Kristie had taken on a local franchise for the Visiting Angels homecare group. She organised home help for the elderly and disabled, or those needing support following medical treatment. Kristie worked hard, and made a comfortable living. The was enhanced by the money she had inherited from Bruce and she continued to heap goodies onto her daughter, including buying Taylor her own horses. But she was also becoming concerned with her daughter's lack of progress at school, and with the friends she was making. Perhaps it was a classic single mother reaction. On the one hand, Kristie wanted her daughter to grow up, and to take responsibility for herself. On the other, she wanted to compensate for the lack of a father figure, and to (as best as she could) replace Bruce in her daughter's affections, to become both mum and dad.

Taylor graduated from Copley High, having gained little in the way of either life skills or qualifications. She lacked all kinds of motivation, and lived off her mother at home, and visiting an increasingly undesirable group of friends. It did not take long for drugs to enter the scene, and depression followed. Taylor, it seems from her social media entries, still desperately missed her father – a matter that does not seem to have been addressed with counselling or such like. But her entries also show a girl who loves her mother. On her Myspace page, she refers to missing her 'Pappi', but also speaks in glowing terms of her mother, and her joy at driving the nearly new Ford Focus bought for her. 'Life is tough sometimes,' she wrote on another occasion, 'but the lessons I've learned from this are to appreciate every day, to try and focus on the positive things and to thank God everyday for the blessings He has put in my life.'

But Kristie was struggling with her; she was desperate for daughter to take more responsibility for her life. A mixture of pressure and (almost certainly undeserved) guilt drove a smothering, suffocating affection. 'She overly loved her daughter,' said Kristie's brother, Jerry Buckholder, 'I'm not going to say she smothered her, but Taylor, I'm sure, lived well.'

After pressure from her mother, Taylor enrolled in Akron University, but even this did not drive her out of her emotional low. After just one semester, she left. This brought matters at home to a head. Taylor had by now a relatively stable and long-term relationship with Brian Smith. Kristie did not warm to the man, who was a couple of years older than her daughter. She suspected that Smith, who came from a run-down housing project in another part of the city, was responsible for her daughter's dabble into the drugs world. In the end, she banned him from visiting her home.

It was the final straw for Taylor. The Marks had a beautiful, double fronted detached home in a good part of the city. But she was prepared to give this up and move into Smith's home, which he shared with his mother. This was a tiny, attached house, a fraction of the size of the Marks' place, and in a neighbourhood renowned from crime, where gun attacks were a regular feature.

Smith's mother was not keen on the move. Tammy Smith described Taylor as 'A little bit whiny and spoiled.' She thought the girl was demanding, a little rich kid from the better part of town who thought she had a wide range of entitlements.

For her part, despite the move, Kristie continued to support her daughter. She would drive into the rough part of the neighbourhood in her sparkling new SUV to deliver money, clothes, food or other requirements of her daughter. At the same time, she was trying her best to instil a sense of personal responsibility into her young adopted daughter, often threatening to 'cut her off' from her inheritance if she did not pull herself together.

But in her social media posts, another side of Taylor made itself known. Her vulnerability. Her insecurity. This was a girl suffering from the death of her father not that many years ago, a grief that had not been addressed. Who had moved across the country and been installed in a school where suddenly she could not succeed. A girl who had left home, and was, if the posts are to be believed, missing her mom. But could not admit it. The messages show a girl proud of her mother's work, and success as a businesswoman. A girl who was excited about a promise to be involved in the business, eventually taking it on, once she completed college. But a girl who just did not have the self-esteem, the belief, to do what was necessary to achieve her wishes.

At the same time, Taylor held unreal expectations about her mother's wealth. She thought she had seen a copy of her mother's will, and believed that there was a well filled offshore account, alongside inherited money, savings and property. As the only child, Taylor believed she was to be the sole beneficiary when her mother passed on. But that was not likely in the immediate future, Kristie was just 58 years old.

In fact, Kristie was nothing like as wealthy as her daughter believed. The offshore account had probably been misread by Taylor and was a trust fund she had set up for her daughter, which would be released over time. Yes, she was comfortably off, but there was not a huge amount of cash around. Much of that had been spent on the youngest member of the family. Most money was tied up in their house and Kristie's business.

On the surface at least, relations between daughter and mother were not good. Taylor was cross at the pressure she was placed under to follow a proper college course, she was angry that her boyfriend was banned from their house, the spoiled, selfish girl was dominating over the more loving and sensitive personality hidden below. She was annoyed by the threats of her mother to cut her out of the will.

In a way not unlike many teenagers and young people in their early twenties, Taylor sounded off to co-workers at the grocery store where she earned some pocket money from her part time work. She would live to regret those not thought through words, as witnesses reported that Taylor had expressed a wish to 'kill' her mother, and had suggested that a colleague should run her down with her van. How seriously the suggestion was made is impossible to prove now, but as a comment, it is not something unusual to hear from a rebellious young person.

This notion of 'killing Kristie Marks' also arose between Taylor, her boyfriend Brian Smith, and his friend Troy Purdie. The questions which have never been fully addressed are who initiated the suggestions, who drove them forwards and how seriously they were meant.

Even the police, however, felt that there was not murderous intention at the beginning. That it was just juvenile talk that went on. And on. Until it became more than a bad taste laugh, and turned into reality.

In October 2009, Taylor was living with Brian and his mother, but appeared to be getting fed up with the arrangements. Brian's mother, remember, was not especially fond of her son's lover. Taylor was missing her mom, and missing her dogs. She decided that she wanted a break from the cramped lifestyle in a dangerous neighbourhood. The girl contacted her mother once more. Kristie heard the message, and thought that all the advice that had been pushed her way by well meaning relations and friends had been proved wrong. She had been warned not to respond to every one of her daughter's whims, not to visit the dangerous neighbourhood, especially at night.

Indeed, a close friend of Kristie had tried especially hard to warn the doting mother of the risks she was taking. Jeff Sigle said later: 'I kept telling Kristie to think the worst in every situation, you're being conned, you're being duped. I told her to watch out for them, don't tread down there by yourself, don't go looking, don't get lured.' Indeed, Sigle felt that there were definite reasons behind Taylor's decision to move out of her comfortable home into a poverty ridden area. A part of that was the attraction of something totally different to what she was used to living. But he suspected that there could be a more sinister plan. 'For a girl who went from having everything she wats to living in that kind of situation, there's got to be a reason. It just doesn't happen, and it doesn't happen overnight,' he continued.

But now Taylor had contacted her, and asked to be collected and taken home. Relief must have rushed through Kristie's arteries – things were finally looking up. She had often told her friends that things would come right in the end. Taylor, for all her frustrating behaviour, needed support, and now she was coming home to get it. At around 8.00pm on the evening of October 24th, Kristie's car was caught on local security CCTV arriving at the project, and pulling into a parking lot close to Smith's home.

Taylor was indoors playing Monopoly with Brian and Troy, along with Tammy Smith. The mother later described them as having a relaxed and cheerful evening, in which a few beers had been consumed.

The next set of events are undisputed. Kristie came to the door, and went inside while Taylor collected her bag. Then, the two left, accompanied by Brian. They walked towards the SUV, parked just a short distance away.

And that was when the murder occurred. A man rushed around the corner, pushing (according to reports) Brian and Taylor aside. The assailant thrust Kristie over a low wall then pounced on her prone body, stabbing her no less than sixteen times.

But from there, matters are less clear. Taylor and Brian claimed that the boyfriend chased the attacker away, but not before he had turned on Brian. Brian gave chase, but he was a large man, who suffered from asthma, and he soon gave up. Troy then appeared on the scene and continued the attempt to catch the attacker.

Meanwhile, a distraught Taylor went into her temporary home and phoned the emergency services. She reported that her mother had been attacked, and was now lying unable to move in the parking lot. The girl was almost incomprehensible in her grief, with the operator trying hard to calm her down and find out what exactly had happened. 'My mother has been stabbed in the parking lot,' she sobbed to the dispatcher. 'Someone just ran up behind my mom and stabbed her.' In the end, Tammy took over the call. She reported how she had heard a scream, and looked through the window to see Kristie collapsed on the floor.

Within a short time, the police and ambulance arrived. Kristie was rushed to hospital, but she died without regaining consciousness.

It is at this point that facts become even more confused. And we also have to debate the actions of the police. We have a just orphaned girl, someone who lost her father and had just witnessed the murder of her mother. We have a man attacked by a killer, who gave chase (as far as is known) with all the adrenalin and stress this involves. Were the police's actions inspired investigative work, catching the culprits when they were at their most vulnerable? Or was it heartless cruelty, which would not have happened had the murder been in the middle-class district in which Kristie lived? Was it an investigation that bullied the culprits into revealing only half truths, meaning the full truth will now never come to light?

Impossible to say, although at worst the police at least got lucky.

Quickly, the investigating officers decided that it was an unusual crime. If a robbery, why had nothing been taken? Kristie's handbag had been snatched, but it was found nearby, untouched. Inside was her purse with a small amount of cash, her phone, credit cards and the keys to her brand new car. Why also had the attacker tackled Kristie, when

Brian, young and big, would present the biggest danger? Surely, the police reasoned, he should have been disabled first?

The police interviewed all four witnesses at Tammy's home, speaking to them in separate rooms so that they could not communicate. It seems an unsympathetic response given what they knew at the time, which was very little.

But the officers thought that they found a weakness in the stories. Detective Pasheilich felt that the answers to questions seemed too unified between Taylor, Brian and Troy. It was as though they had been rehearsed.

It was unclear, also, why Troy had left the house. That evening, just hours after the attack, Troy, Brian and Taylor were taken to the police station to face questioning and to give DNA, so that they could be 'eliminated as suspects.' But the questioning was tough, not sympathetic at all. The police clearly believed that they had their killers, and were determined to prove it. On this occasion, it appears as though they were right. Had they been wrong, then who knows what psychological harm may have been caused?

Perhaps there is a very fine line between brilliant police work, and irresponsible investigation. Brian Smith was spoken to first, then Troy. Taylor Marks was left to stew. When it was her turn, she was pushed hard on a description of the killer. James had identified a red bandana, which had been found near Kristie's handbag. Taylor tried to describe the loose braids in the attacker's hair, similar to those worn by Troy Purdie. The detectives suggested that the killer was, in fact, Troy. And that she had asked him to kill her mother on a number of occasions.

Almost hysterical, Taylor confirmed that indeed the killer was Troy. He was then brought in, and played the tape in which he was identified. Troy collapsed quickly, and confirmed that he had carried out the act. When asked why, he said that he was to be paid $5000, then would leave the area. The money would come from Taylor Marks.

Presented with that story, Taylor denied any desire to kill her mother. She said that she loved her mom. She stated that she had no money, certainly not enough to find $5000. 'But you would have had it soon,' the detectives argued.

Given the pressure of the two confessions, Smith (when interviewed again) asked for the recorder to be turned off. He then, it is claimed, confirmed that the murder had been planned, and the idea had been Taylor's. She wanted her mother's money, and that desire overpowered any other feelings she held for her parent.

Within four hours of the crime being committed, the police had three heads on a plate. A good night's work, they felt. Under Ohio law, not only is murder a capital offence, but paying someone to carry out the crime is also considered worthy of the death penalty. It looked as though both Troy Purdie and Taylor Marks would be facing the electric chair.

Their situation was made worse when local CCTV footage came into the hands of the police. There were many cameras on the project, such were the crime rates, and one was covering the main parking lot. Although pictures were distant, they clearly showed the arrival of Kristie's car. Then, a few minutes later, three figures are seen heading from the direction of Tammy's house towards the lot. Another figure runs into shot, pushes over Kristie, and stabs her. The figure's arm is seen rising and falling rhythmically, its very lack of frenzy making it an even more chilling sight.

Two other people are seen standing and watching. One is large, and is almost certainly Smith, the other frailer figure has to be Taylor. They are doing nothing to stop the assault, and their body language does not support their initial claims that they were attempting to halt the attack, even verbally. Smith had said that he had approached the attacker a couple of times, drawing his attention and getting wounded himself into the bargain. But the wounds on his head and finger are minor, and partially healed. They are not in line with slashes from the large carving knife police later found, covered in Kristie's blood. Taylor had said that she had screamed at the attacker to stop, and certainly Tammy said that she had heard screams – not too unusual in the particular neighbourhood of Springdale Drive, Akron. But the CCTV footage disputes that she had tried to stop the attack. She is standing still, arms on her sides, apparently watching the murder.

A one-million-dollar bond was placed on each of the three accused, and they were held in custody at the Summit County Jail. With Purdie and Marks held under the State's Murder for Hire statutes, only Smith was not facing the death penalty, being charged with the slightly less serious aggravated murder for his involvement in the plot.

The police decided within a week of the arrests that the motivation for the crime was financial, with Taylor expecting to inherit a small fortune from her mother. Indeed, she was named as the sole beneficiary of Kristie's personal property and life insurance monies. The bulk of the savings was to be placed in a trust for Taylor, but police suspected that she did not know this, thinking that it would all come immediately to her. 'She believed it would leave her sitting pretty,' Detective Parhelic told local reporters at the time.

'Taylor mentioned that her mom has money and has a will and that she believes that her name's on the will because she saw it. More or less, it comes down to money,' he continued.

But with the three suspects behind bars, confessions neatly collected, matters began to change. The prosecutors began to suspect that public opinion would not tolerate the death sentence placed on a young girl from a background which included the devastating loss of her father. If Marks could not be sent to the electric chair, then the same had to be said for Purdie.

In the time of reflection, Marks also told a slightly different version of events. In these, it was Brian Smith who had driven the crime. What had started out as silly, tasteless joking had sparked an interest in his mind, and he had been the one to apply pressure on Taylor to carry out the crime – which he knew his friend would enact – and find the $5000 fee Troy Purdie would require. Things had moved so quickly immediately after the crime that, Taylor Marks said, she had not been able to think. She was also afraid of telling the truth if there were a chance that he could get at her.

She revealed this to the police who had investigated the crime, and asked them for a plea bargain. The chief prosecutor was informed, and felt that, on balance, a guilty plea from the two facing the death penalty would mean life imprisonment without the chance of parole would be enough.

In under a year from the date of the crime, the 21-year-old Taylor Marks was in court. Tearful, pale and generally unhealthy looking the young woman admitted offering $5000 to Troy Purdie to murder her mother. She says that she did not understand the gravity of what they were discussing, and then her mental state was so unbalanced that she did not feel able to pull out of the plans. She told the court that she was willing to testify against the others involved. That proved unnecessary, because the men also pleaded guilty, each accepting a term of life imprisonment without the possibility of parole.

The prosecutors requested the dismissal of the death penalty specification in the crime, and the judge, Tom Parker, reluctantly agreed, although he told the family that it was not a decision he had found easy to make. The family, too, believed that Kristie would never want her daughter executed. It was help that she would want for her girl, not death.

'You will never again enjoy the freedom that the rest of us take for granted,' Parker told the distraught Taylor, announcing the sentence.

And so, a young lady spends the remainder of her life behind bars. A child who had grown up with seemingly everything until, in the space of a few years, the triple hit of the death of father, moving cross country and school failure hit her so hard. Was this a crime about money, as the police claim? Maybe, but more probably a tragedy whose seeds contained far more complicated DNA than simple greed.

BABY KILLER
The True Story of Amelia Dyer

Chrissy Eubank

AMELIA DYER

Amelia Dyer, considered one of the most prolific serial killers in history, was born around 1837 in Victorian Britain. Her picture on the front cover easily betrays the evil that resided within her heart. Her reign of terror lasted over twenty years, as she is projected to have killed as many as 400 children before finally being caught

She embarked on a thirty year career of killing with eyewitnesses seeing at least six babies entering her house a day. The count of 400 dead is a conservative estimate.

EARLY LIFE

Amelia was the youngest of five children born into the tiny town of Pyle Marsh. She had three older brothers, Thomas, James, and William along with an older sister named Ann. Her father was a shoemaker named Samuel Hobley and her mother was named Sarah Weymouth.

But he didn't come from an impoverished family like so many others during the Victorian Era.

"For the time, she had a pretty good start," said author Allison Rattle. "Her father had a pretty good trade and paid for her to go to church and school which at the time only a quarter of the children her age actually got an education so she was privileged in that respect."

She found entertainment in reading and used to write poetry herself. Amelia's mother Sarah, however, became mentally ill after suffering from typhus fever. Amelia had to suffer through watching her mother's seizures and outbursts, providing care for her until she died in 1848.

"She witnessed her mother basically losing her mind," said Rattle. "And dying a slow, horrific death. I guess being a young girl she may have been called upon to nurse her mother slightly or at least wait upon her."

Psychologists have posited that it was going through this trauma of watching her mother lose her mind, that caused Amelia's own emotional wiring to run askew.

"Amelia would later claim that her mother died as a result of hereditary insanity," said author Allison Vale. "I think though that this isn't true but it's really easy to understand how she could have remembered it that way."

"It was certain to have a massive impact on her and she may have learned a few things about what kind of symptoms might be shown by someone whose losing their mind."

Amelia was sent to live with her aunt in nearby Bristol after her mother's death. She started an apprenticeship with a corset maker and worked there until her father died in 1859. The oldest brother, Thomas, took control of the family shoe business.

Two years later, some type of estrangement occurred with her brothers, specifically James and Amelia doesn't appear to have further ties with her family.

In 1861, Amelia moved to Trinity Street, Bristol. She married George Thomas, who at 59 years old was 35 years Amelia's senior. The two lied about their ages on their marriage certificate with George claiming he was 48 years old and Amelia claiming she was 30.

A CAREER IN "HEALTH CARE"

Amelia began training as a nurse after she got married.

"Amelia turned to one of the most arduous professions she could have turned to," Vale said. "Nursing was just starting to change. It was post-Crimean war. Nursing was starting to have a much better profile as a result of Florence Nightingale. But it was still a thankless profession."

"It wasn't a caring profession like it is present day," agreed psychologist Laura Richards. "They train you psychologically to be a lot more robust around dealing with people. So she became quite hardy and emotionless from having been trained through the nursing regime."

Amelia became pregnant at the age of twenty-six before she met a woman named Ellen Dane who came to boarder at her house. Dane was a midwife who told her of a lucrative and shady way to earn money. Amelia would use her own home as a front to provide housing for women who had gotten pregnant out of wedlock. They would them give the babies away for adoption or kill them through malnutrition.

They called it baby farming.

"Amelia could see it was a very easy way to make money," Rattle said. "Although with risks involved obviously although Amelia did have training as a mid-wife as well through her nursing experience so it was certainly something she knew she was capable of doing. That was the beginning of a massive change in Amelia's life."

Dane moved her base of operations to the USA while Amelia took her "business plan" to heart. During this time, unmarried mothers did not have access to any kind of subsidy as the 1834 Poor Law Amendment Act did not oblige the fathers of illegitimate children to pay for their upbringing. These laws, coupled with the stigmatization of single mothers, forced the practice of baby farming.

Amelia discussed business strategies with Dane. She knew the best bet was to insist on being paid upfront with a one-time fee. She refused any type of money for continuous care as she knew that would mean the mother would return to visit.

"The one off premiums were certainly not enough to sustain a child's life for long financially," Vale said. "And the only way that it would be profitable for a baby farmer was to subject a child to persist underfeeding that would at some point bring about the infant's death."

"Abortion was not an option," Judith Knelman said. "So the simplest thing to do was hide, have the baby and get rid of it. Pay somebody to take care of it or pay somebody to get rid of it."

The babies were subsequently left on the premises and seen as "nurse children."

"Illegitimacy was seen as hugely immoral," said author Allison Rattle. "Even orphanages would only accept orphans from families where the parents were married and the father had died. They wouldn't accept a child who was born out of wedlock."

"Dickens did a really good job of describing social conditions in the 1850 and 60s," Knelman added. "Certainly there were a lot of poor people. There were a lot of neglected and abandoned children."

"There was no work," said Alan McCormick of Scotland Yard. "There was no social services. There was no welfare. One in every twelve women was a prostitute. A child being born in normal circumstances only had a fifty percent chance of reaching the age of five. So that's how bad it was."

BABY FARMING

"Baby farming was a business carried out throughout the country," said historian Ken Wells. "If a mother was unable to look after their child, there was an option of sending them out to a baby farmer, also known as fostering, with the understanding that they could visit the child whenever they wanted to."

On the surface they were providing a service to a growing need. They took an unwanted child and gave them to a foster parent. Only those foster parents and caregivers didn't always have the best interests of the infant at heart.

"MOTHER'S FRIEND"

The majority of these "caregivers" resorted to starving out the babies. They sedated crying babies with alcohol or drugs usually using Godfrey's Cordial, also known as 'Mother's Friend'. This syrup was one of the most popular medicines given to infants and children in both the United States and England in the latter years of the 18th and early 19th centuries. The syrup was used as a panacea to everything from colic to jaundice to excessive crying to diarrhea. 'Mother's Friend' was harmful despite its harmless sounding name as it contained one grain of opium for every two ounces. Many infants were poisoned from this syrup which was administered in secret by nurses who wanted to keep babies under their care in a deep state of sleep and thus more manageable.

"A hungry child, a noisy child, is a difficult child to raise," author Allison Vale said. "And something that was chillingly referred to colloquially as 'the Quietness' was an over the counter anti-colic cordial and it did contain liquid opium which was laudanum and in some cases brandy."

"People gave babies laudanum when they were supposed to be giving them food," Klansman said. "Because it dulled the need, or dulled the awareness of the baby that it was hungry. Of course it didn't nourish the baby so eventually a baby that was given that and not given enough food would die."

The babies would die from severe malnutrition but the coroner would record the death as "debility from birth", "lack of breast milk" or "starvation."

There were those guilt-ridden mothers who returned to the baby-farming homes to check on their children but would find their efforts blocked. Most would be too scared or embarrassed to inform the police of any wrongdoing. The police themselves had numerous problems tracking any children that were deemed missing.

"Dead infants," Vale said. "Or abandoned infants were as commonplace in British cities as roadkill today. Babies were found parceled up in railroad stations, under railroad arches."

"It was desperation," McCormick added. "For the vast majority of these ladies."

TO A MANNER BORN

With Dane's departure to the States, Amelia set her sights on taking her place in the baby-farming business. She had just given birth to her own daughter, Ellen, but in 1869 her husband George died.

A widow at age 32 with a baby, Amelia needed a new source of income...

She began taking in pregnant women as she placed ads to nurse and adopt the babies. In return, she required a large one-time fee and clothing for the child. She began meeting with expectant young women, convincing them that she was someone who could be trusted in providing a safe and loving home for their child.

Before she followed through with her plan, however, she put her own child up for adoption and sent her away.

"It was a choice that she made," Vale said. "She had options. She could have worked through. But instead what she does is to farm her own child out and opt for the easy money that she seemed to be able to make."

"As Amelia chose to go into the baby farming business," Rattle said. "She was maybe able to travel around here, there and everywhere adopting babies so it made sense for her daughter to be out of the way."

Three years after her first husband George died, Amelia remarried. His name was William Dyer, a brewers laborer from Bristol. They had two children together, Mary Ann aka Polly and William Samuel.

Amelia eventually left William, however, as the latter lost his job and offered little in the way of finances.

Strapped for cash, Amelia decided to dispense with the heavy cost of letting the babies die through neglect and starvation. So after each child was born she promptly murdered them, thus incurring a windfall of profits.

"Baby farmers used different methods," Klansman said. "Some of which are less palatable than others."

"Quite often she would suffocate babies at birth," Rattle said. "Smothering the baby the moment its head came out, before it turned blue as that would be a sign that it had taken its first breath. (She made) it would look like a stillbirth so the death certificate would all be above board."

When her daughter Polly asked why so many babies came and disappeared, Amelia described herself as the "angel maker."

"I'm sending little children to Jesus," Amelia said. "Because he wanted them far more than their mothers did."

"Cold," Alan McCormick of New Scotland Yard said in describing Amelia. "Those kids meant nothing to her. It was just a means of getting money."

It can be argued, however, that once Amelia got a taste of killing she did it more for the power than the money and greed.

"The actual killing of the child," Holmes said. "Watching the child peacefully to some degree die. It parallels perhaps seeing her mother pass away where she felt an almost God-like power over these children that she had decided were going to go to their maker."

AROUSING SUSPICION

"Amelia was already aware of the fact that this was not going to be about her helping children," forensic psychologist David Holmes said. "This was going to be a fairly cruel and anti-mothering act that would be carried out in order to gain all of this money."

Amelia successfully avoided police involvement until 1879, a good ten years into her murderous ways. A doctor became suspicious about the number of child deaths he had been called in to certify under Amelia's care.

"The inquests were held in Somerset," Vale said. "And they're (the police) pretty certain that the babies have died as a direct result of neglect and opium overdose. But they can't prove it. And interestingly, she gets off with a six months sentence with hard labor."

Without a coroner that was able to rule completely against her, Amelia would have undoubtedly been executed by hanging.

"Its incredibly really," Rattle said. "That she only got six months. And there was one example, we read of a chap who got twelve months for stealing a piece of bacon."

Amelia took the punishment hard, becoming an emotional wreck during her jail stay. She resumed her business, however, as soon as she was released.

"In the long term," Holmes reasoned. "It mostly would have served as a very hard lesson in forensic awareness that she wasn't gonna get caught again. And there was no way she was going to leave any evidence which had been the problem in leading up to her capture."

She was sent to mental hospitals for supposed mental illness and suicidal ideations but these seemed to be well-timed acts. From her experience of working in an asylum, Amelia knew the tricks of the trade in order to make her stay an easy one.

"I don't think Amelia Dyer was insane," said Vale. "I think she was a very bad person who deliberately committed murder for profit."

Amelia had both an alcohol and substance abuse problem, using on a regular basis as she began her killings once again.

"Certainly the drugs would have had an impact on her," Richards said. "On her mental state. Maybe induced this complete detachment from reality."

"A long term laudanum habit," Vale concurred. "Will lead to periods of depression. It can lead to mood swings even when you're not under the influence. I think it also exacerbates any underlying mental health issues."

RETURNING TO BABY FARMING

In 1884, British society took a much harder line against baby farming and any sign of neglect or abuse would be reported.

"She definitely changes her modus operandi at this point (after 1884)," Vale said. "She's beginning to murder these children."

In 1890, Amelia took on the care of the illegitimate baby of a governess. She had begun targeting the babies of the more affluent because of the larger amounts of money involved. The higher up the social class the woman was, however, the more risk was involved as the woman may have means to question and come after Amelia.

"This was a young governess who fell in love with the young master of the house that she worked in and had got pregnant," Rattle said. "She was left on her own and she responds to an advert, gets in touch with Amelia Dyer and moves in with her. Amelia was able to gain the trust of this woman as with many others, so much so that the governess was persuaded to leave her baby in the care of Amelia once it was born."

The governess, however, returned to visit her baby months later and immediately became suspicious that the child she was given was not hers. She stripped the baby to see if a birth mark was present on one of its hips. It wasn't and the governess immediately informed the authorities.

The police, however, could never pin Amelia down.

"She managed to put them off time and time again by sending them on wild goose chases," Rattle said. "She said she had sent them to a couple that moved here...that moved there."

Amelia continued to move from town to town but still found herself being stalked by the governess who wouldn't give up.

"She did feel hounded," Richards said. "I'm sure that would have had an impact on her. She would have felt that pressure."

Amelia then feigned another nervous breakdown and a doctor was brought in. "The birds are telling me to do it! The birds are telling me to do it!" she would cry out, forcing the doctor to send her to an asylum.

"She was a very clever lady," Holmes said. "With the police getting close to her and she needed to lose herself and what better place to go than somewhere like that (a mental asylum)."

Her mental illness continued on unabated as she drank two bottles of laudanum in an attempted suicide. Her long term use of opium, however, allowed her to build up the tolerance necessary to survive.

"Amelia would be drawn to the idea of self-medicating," Holmes said. "Possibly seeing it as a route, a means to ease the situation, make it even easier for her to put up with what she was doing."

"She took it (opium) on a regular basis," Richards said. "She took it almost daily so she was an addict. So that would induce a form of state from her mentally where she would be detached from reality and I think that was part of her coping mechanism to detach from the reality of what she was doing."

After that close call and subsequent hospital release, Amelia resumed baby farming and murder.

"Her mental breakdowns were very short lived," Richards noted. "She would be out of sorts for a period of time that get it all back together again. To me that would say there isn't a mental illness there."

A CLEVER KILLER

She wised up to doing things on the books and decided to stop getting doctors to issue death certificates. Amelia decided to kill and bury the bodies herself. In order to do this, she would have to be a killer on the run as inevitably the mothers would come back seeking to reclaim their children or check on their welfare. Amelia took her family to different cities to escape suspicion as soon as things got too hot. She would use a series of different aliases and rename her businesses.

"Amelia committed what many serial killers do," Holmes explained. "The mistake of accelerating and being over enthusiastic. Either for reasons that she was enjoying the process or quite simply greed was driving her over the edge."

Baby farming began to gain the attention and compassion of the British ruling class, however. They asked why if they had laws for the prevention of the cruelty of animals then why didn't there laws protecting children. With the arrest and hanging of Margaret Waters (another baby farming killer) and the fleeing Dyer, Amelia's colleagues were going downhill fast and perhaps she thought her time was limited.

By 1893, Amelia had another breakdown but was released from the Wells mental asylum. This would be the last time she would be hospitalized. She moved to Caversham, Berkshire with a woman named Jane "Granny" Smith who didn't know of Amelia's exploits.

"She befriends an old lady named Jane Smith," Vale said. "She's widowed and resigned to spend her last days in the workhouse. Amelia seduces her with stories of rescuing the unwanted infants. Of nursing them. And it's a very, very seductive image. And Jane Smith buys into it, wholesale."

Her daughter Mary Ann aka Polly and her husband Arthur Palmer came along as well.

The group moved to 45 Kensington Road, Reading Berkshire in that same year. Amelia had the perfect front. She coached Jane Smith to call her "mother" in front of prospective clients while Amelia would call her "Granny."

A ruse to project a mother-daughter image and put the guards down of the pregnant young women.

"Jane Smith didn't get the life she was promised at all," Rattle said. "She was treated as no more than a servant really. She was made to look after the children, to clean the house."

Amelia then puts her adoptions into overdrive. The babies come in and out of the house with such rapidity that old lady Jane Smith doesn't even learn their names.

Eyewitnesses later claimed that there were six infants a day coming to and from the house daily.

THE MURDERS CONTINUE

The advertisement in the "Miscellaneous" column of the Bristol Times & Mirror newspaper was poignant.

In January of 1896 a popular barmaid named Evelina Marmon gave birth to a daughter out of wedlock. She named the baby Doris and she sought immediately to have it adopted. She placed an ad in the "Miscellaneous" section of the Bristol Times & Mirror newspaper.

"Wanted, respectable woman to take young child." Marmon intended to go back to work and hoped to eventually reclaim her child.

Evelina was a God-fearing farmer's daughter who left the farm for city life. She found work as a barmaid in the saloon of the Plough Hotel, an old coaching inn. She was buxom with blonde hair and had a vibrant personality. She had plenty of suitors and became pregnant by one of the male patrons who left her deserted.

Evelina knew she could not bring up the baby on her own.

She would have to find a foster home for little Doris - to have her "adopted out", in the language of the time - go back to work and hope in time to be able to reclaim her child.

Next to her own ad was an advertisement that read *"Married couple with no family would adopt healthy child, nice country home. Terms, £10".*

Marmon answered the ad which was addressed to a "Mrs. Harding", an alias of Amelia. A few days later Amelia wrote back, saying *"I should be glad to have a dear little baby girl, one I could bring up and call my own. We are plain, homely people, in fairly good circumstances. I don't want a child for money's sake, but for company and home comfort... Myself and my husband are dearly fond of children. I have no child of my own. A child with me will have a good home and a mother's love. It is just lovely here, heatlhy and pleasant. There is an orchard opposite our front door."*

Evelina was assured that she could visit whenever she wished.

"Rest assured I will do my duty by that dear child. I will be a mother, as far as lies in my power."

"It is just lovely here, healthy and pleasant. There is an orchard opposite our front door."

Evelina tried to negotiate a weekly fee for the care of Doris but Amelia wanted a substantial one-time fee to be paid upfront. Evelina, seemingly with no other choice, agreed to pay the £10, and a week later "Mrs Harding" arrived in Cheltenham.

Evelina was surprised that Amelia aka "Mrs. Harding" was old (59 years) and heavy set (over 210 lbs). She remained reluctant at first but gave in as the elderly woman immediately showed her Doris some affection, covering her with a shawl.

Evelina gave the old lady a cardboard box of clothes she had prepared – nappies, chemises, petticoats, frocks, nightgowns, and a powder box. She also enclosed the money and received a signed receipt from "Mrs.Harding."

She accompanied her baby daughter and her eventual killer to Cheltenham station then on to Gloucester. Evelina stood there crying through the hot steam on the platform as the 5:20 p.m train took her baby away.

When Evelina returned home, she described herself as "a broken woman."

Days later, she received a letter from "Mrs. Harding" offering her assurance that all was well with her daughter. Evelina wrote back but received no replies afterward.

Amelia told Evelina that she would be going to Reading but lied. She traveled to 76 Mayo Road, Willesden, London where her daughter Mary Ann was staying. Amelia then took some white edging tape and wrapped it around the baby's neck, making a strangling knot. The baby did not die immediately.

"I used to like to watch them with the tape around their neck," Amanda said. "But it was soon all over with them."

"The idea of strangling and using the tape may make it seem almost symbolical or bizarre to ourselves," Holmes said. "But in terms of criminal awareness she was aware of the fact that if she tried to suffocate a baby its not always absolutely certain that the baby is dead."

The mother and daughter team wrapped the baby up with a napkin. They kept the clothes that Evelina gave her and hoped to sell it to a pawnbroker. Amelia used some of the money to pay the rent to her landlady and gave the woman a pair of child's boots as a present for her own little girl.

The following day, April 1st of 1896, a young boy named Harry Simmons was taken to the Mayo Road residence. Amelia had no spare white edging tape available and used the tape from Doris' corpse to strangle the year old boy.

The next day both bodies were rolled into a carpet bag, their corpses stacked one on top of the other. Bricks were added inside for additional weight. Amelia headed back toward Reading, taking the bus to Paddington and then the train. She dragged the carpet bag through the streets until she reached the River Thames. She had a secluded spot at Caversham Lock and she forced the carpet bag through the railing and didn't leave until she heard it splash into the waters below.

She didn't know she had a witness as a man passed, hurrying on his way home calling out "Good night."

A SHOCKING DISCOVERY

Ironically, only days before the dumping of the bodies a package was fished out of the Thames by a bargeman. This package was the work of Amelia as she had not weighed it down adequately. It contained the body of a baby girl named Helena Fry. With only a small police force available in Reading, a Constable Anderson made a significant discovery. He found a label from Temple Meads Station, Bristol and he used microscopic analysis of the wrapping paper. He found a faintly legible name. A "Mrs.Thomas" and an address.

The address of Amelia Dyer.

The police immediately placed Amelia's home under surveillance. They did enough research on Amelia and knew that she would "disappear" if she thought she was under suspicion. So they decided they would be better served if they would use a young woman as a decoy to secure a meeting with Amelia and discuss the prospect of using her "adoptive services."

On April 3rd, while Amelia was waiting on the decoy to arrive, she answered the door to a police raid. The smell of decomposing bodies radiated throughout her home but no human remains were found. The police found other evidence, however, such as the white edging tape, telegrams describing adoption arrangements, pawn tickets for children's clothing, receipts for newspaper ads and letters from distraught mothers asking about the welfare of their child.

The police determined that in the few months Amelia had been in Reading at least twenty children had been placed into her care. She had been preparing to move again, this time to the town of Somerset.

Amelia was arrested on April 4th, three days after the murders of Doris Marmon and Harry Simmons. The Thames River was searched and six more bodies were discovered, including Doris and Harry.

Each child had been strangled with the seamstress white tape and Amelia later told police that "was how you could tell it was one of mine."

Eleven days later, Evelina Marmon had been contacted by police as they found her name in items found in Amelia's home. Distraught, she came to identify her daughter's remains.

THE TRIAL OF A KILLER

An inquest was held a month later. Amelia's daughter Mary Ann and her husband Arthur were not charged as there was no direct evidence that they were her accomplices. Arthur was set free because of a confession handwritten by Amelia. She wrote:

Sir will you kindly grant me the favour of presenting this to the magistrates on Saturday the 18th instant I have made this statement out, for I may not have the opportunity then I must relieve my mind I do know and I feel my days are numbered on this earth but I do feel it is an awful thing drawing innocent people into trouble I do know I shal have to answer before my Maker in Heaven for the awful crimes I have committed but as God Almighty is my judge in Heaven a on Hearth neither my daughter Mary Ann Palmer nor her husband Alfred Ernest Palmer I do most solemnly declare neither of them had any thing at all to do with it, they never knew I contemplated doing such a wicked thing until it was to late I am speaking the truth and nothing but the truth as I hope to be forgiven, I myself and I alone must stand before my Maker in Heaven to give an answer for it all witnes my hand

Amelia Dyer.

— April 16, 1896

On May 22nd, 1896, Amelia appeared in court and pleaded guilty to the murder of Doris Marmon. Her family and friends testified that they had their own suspicions about Amelia and spoke of times that she evaded discovery. A man came forth claiming he had seen and spoken to Amelia as she had disposed of two bodies at Caversham Lock proved key to the prosecution.

Amelia used insanity as a defense, offering her stays in mental asylums as proof of her instability. The prosecution, however, argued that her symptoms were well-rehearsed actions to avoid suspicion as both of her hospital stays coincided with times that Amelia felt her murders would be discovered.

The jury took four and a half minutes to find her guilty. Amelia then spent three weeks in her condemned cell, filling five journals with her confessions. A chaplain visited her the night before her execution and asked if she had anything to confess. She offered him her journals, asking "isn't this enough?"

Amelia was then subpoenaed to appear as a witness in her daughter's own trial for murder which was set for a week after her own execution date. The court ruled, however, that Amelia became "legally dead" after she was sentenced and her testimony would be inadmissible.

On the day of her execution, Amelia discovered that the charges against her daughter had been dropped.

On June 10th, 1896, Amelia Dyer was hanged by James Billington at Newgate Prison. Asked on the scaffold if she had anything to say, she said "I have nothing to say."

URBAN LEGEND?

It remains unknown as to why Amelia's daughter Mary Ann aka Polly was never convicted. Her own daughter provided the majority of the testimony that procured the conviction of her mother but nothing is said about her own involvement.

And the baby murders did not stop after Amelia's death.

Two years after her execution, railroad workers inspecting carriages found a parcel tied up with a string inside a siding on the Plymouth express.

Inside was a three-week old baby girl. The infant was shivering and wet...but alive.

A little research showed that the baby was the child of a widow named Jane Hill. Hill had given the baby to a woman named "Mrs. Stewart" for the one time fee of £12.

"The little one would have a good home and a parent's love and care," Mrs. Stewart had written, her prose eerily echoing that of Amelia Dyer. "Mrs. Stewart" had picked up the baby at Plymouth and dumped her on the next train.

The conjecture was that "Mrs. Stewart" was none other than Polly, Amelia's daughter.

SATAN'S DAUGHTER

28

THE TRUE STORY OF NATASHA CORNETT

29

TRISH SAMUELSON

Natasha Cornett was born January 26th, 1979 in Pikeville, Kentucky.

Pikeville is located in the foothills of the Appalachian mountains. It is a mining town with most of its inhabitants devoutly religious.

"It's very beautiful scenery to grow up in," Cornett said. "But it's a suffocating place to live."

Born poor, Natasha was the product of an affair between her mother Madonna Wallen and her biological father, a police officer named Roger Burgess.

Her mother then left her husband, Ed Wallen, and raised Natasha alone. They lived in a trailer in Pikeville, Kentucky.

"She had energy to burn," her mother said. "She liked to draw. To read. She liked dogs and babies."

SCHOOL LIFE

Natasha was a good student in elementary school, behaving well and getting good grades. She seemed to be on the right path until one morning she found her mother laying unconscious. Madonna Wallen had overdosed on prescription drugs.

"My momma is on the bed naked," Cornett recalled. "With a bottle of pills laying next to her. I didn't know she was dying. It messed with me."

Around this time, Cornett's life began a downward spiral. She began suffering from anorexia. Then drugs. Then she began engaging in acts of self-mutilation, cutting her arms to "relieve her pain."

"Natasha started to engage in those acts as a means of getting control," forensic psychologist Roberta Nixon said. "She can control her diet. She can control her anger, or so she thinks, by cutting herself. She can control how she feels by doing drugs. Having a dim-witted mother certainly didn't help things either."

At one point, Natasha had lost over thirty pounds because of her anorexia as well as having over seventy cuts on her arms.

"I started cutting because I started going through a rough time with my mom," Natasha said. "It was a release."

"I don't know where that pain comes from," Natasha's mother, Madonna Wallen said. "She just says she has to do it to take away her pain."

In later court testimony, however, Wallen would admit to a history of physical abuse with her daughter.

"I used a belt one time and the buckles slipped from my hand," Wallen said. "And it hit her on the back of the leg. But it made a bruise on her."

Wallen later said that there was sexual abuse of Natasha by her husband whom she originally believed to be Natasha's father.

"Natasha had a really bad upbringing," C. Berkeley Bell, the District Attorney General for Tennessee said. "Lot of hard times. She came from a very dysfunctional family. Hard time in school. Was an outcast. Was ostracized by her classmates."

HIGH SCHOOL DROPOUT

Natasha entered high school but dropped out before her freshman year was complete. Her best friend was Karen Howell who would later be part of the "Wild Bunch" that Cornett would lead on a killing spree.

"Karen was my life raft," Natasha said. "She was the only person that understood me and let me be me. She knew my pain. She went through the same stuff."

Like Natasha, Karen had a dysfunctional family. Her father was an abusive alcoholic and her mother had a nervous breakdown. She came from a strict, religious family with her mother forcing her to stand on a Bible when she misbehaved. She was also bipolar.

"They were like two peas in a pod," Nixon said. "But in court interviews Natasha seems to more of a realization of what took place that night. Karen remained a petulant teenager, sullen and angry. Natasha was the better talker of the two so Karen followed her lead.

BIPOLAR DISORDER

Natasha was eventually diagnosed with bipolar disorder and in one episode had to be hospitalized at the Ridge Treatment Center in

Lexington, KY. She had to leave the hospital after eleven days, however, as that was all the time the state health benefits would allow.

"Bipolar disease is brutal and even more so for people in low income circumstances," Nixon said. "It is extremely hard to treat. The amazing thing here is that she was only hospitalized for eleven days. After that, she doesn't appear to have gone through any kind of outpatient treatment program aside from an aborted session with a counselor. With people like Natasha, they need medication to keep their anxiety and impulses under control. Without it, anything can happen and anything will happen."

Natasha's mother began to see the rapid decline in her emotional state. Her choice of clothing would be reflect her mood and growing anger.

"From the seventh grade," Wallen said. "She just started changing. The big baggy pants. The rope with the emblems hanging. Everybody thought it was weird."

"I started drinking and smoking and associating with people that were weird," Natasha said. "You don't have to be perfect around them."

Natasha sought acceptance and eventually found it in the Goth subculture. Still, with the rapid mood shifts and change in dress, Natasha's own mother insists that there are three versions of Natasha.

"There is the sweet, caring girl," Wallen said. "There is the girl who would do anything for her friends, and there is a dark side that likes to play on a Oujia board, do seances and play vampire games."

MARRIAGE

At the age of seventeen, Natasha married Stephen Cornett. It was no ordinary ceremony, however. The bride and groom wore black and dog collars.

"We'd been friends for awhile," Natasha said. "It seemed like the logical thing to do."

The union only lasted a couple of months. Steven left without warning, abandoning Natasha. The dissolution of the marriage caused Natasha to spiral further into depression.

"It was awful," Natasha said. "I just kinda caved in on myself."

Natasha then fully immersed herself in the Goth subculture even further. She donned black clothing and listened intently to the dark, depressing music. She would pierce her eyebrows and lips with safety pins as well as use black lipstick and nail polish.

"For most kids," Nixon said. "The Goth culture is a way to rebel. To control their own image. It is a relatively harmless phase for most involved. They're young. They act out. Then they grow out of it. For some kids, however, like Natasha, it is more than that. She's disturbed to begin with and wants to take it beyond the dark music and black get-ups and really wants to do harm to someone. She realized that the Goth culture was a way to make people afraid of her. This is how she would gain power. She could control people by being their 'darkness consultant.'"

NATASHA THE VAMPIRE

She became a self-described "vampire" and named her black dog "Malkavian" after the vampires in her favorite vampire fantasy board game as well as collecting all of Anne Rice's vampire novels.

"She was a dark soul who'd give you the willies," a local teen said in describing her.

Natasha covered the walls of her bedroom in her trailer with numerous dark messages including "I hate the world" as well as drawing inverted crosses.

"Tasha would start hearing voices," Wallen said. "Talking to people on the Oujia board. Her and Karen fed on each other. You know. It just kept getting worse. She wanted away from all the people that called her 'freak.'"

Her drug use and drinking increased but she was able to attract a group of friends, most of whom looked up to her. The group consisted of three girls. The petite Karen Howell and the overweight, awkward Crystal Sturgill.

Sturgill was molested by her step-father and had been kicked out of her home. She needed a place to stay and hooked up with Karen and Natasha.

The threesome would go around the sleepy Kentucky town, spray painting pentagrams, the satanic number 666 and inverted crosses across the walls of buildings and homes.

"They were all sort of drop outs," reporter Bill Jones said. "Who fell through the cracks in school. They dressed in Gothic fashion, black clothing. Black make-up. Looks Satanic, if you're looking for Satanic that's what might come to mind."

"Everything that we did," Natasha said. "Was very destructive but also self-destructive. Nothing was done to harm anybody but ourselves."

Natasha began spelling her name backwards, 'Ah-Satan', spray painting it across the walls of the town.

"She used the name to intimidate," Dixon said. "In an odd way, that was part of her charm. She was more 'out there' than the impressionable kids in her town. She held sway over Karen Howell and Crystal Sturgill, both of whom were looking for someone they could look up to. So while Natasha was an outcast at school she was able to assemble other outcasts and cast them under her spell. She became the devil of choice to worship."

The gang carried around two books with them, *The Book of Black Magic* and the *Complete Book of Magic and Witchcraft*. The three girls would go to motel rooms or Natasha's mother's trailer to hang out, drink alcohol and each other's blood. They would also engage in seances and Satanic rituals they would read about in books.

"When it comes to the occult," Dixon said. "Most young people just dabble around with it. In the case of Natasha and her gang, however, she led them over the edge. They were dumb kids out looking for kicks and she pushed them into something that they probably would not have gotten involved in had it not been for her own dark compulsions."

ROAD TRIP TO HELL

"We're going to start armageddon," Natasha informed one of her friends. "I hate, therefore I am" became her mantra.

Natasha and the "Wild Bunch" decided to go on a road trip to New Orleans. They were obsessed with the vampire books of Anne Rice and thought about the prospect of meeting her. Talks began and the entire group wanted to leave the small town of Pikeville behind.

"All I could think of was I need out," Natasha said. "I need out. I need out. I need out. I can't breathe, I need out."

The group of girls were now joined by some equally nefarious young men. The first is Joe Risner who is Karen's boyfriend and at twenty years old, the oldest in the group. Risner, never knew his own father and was known as the quiet, introverted type. He wanted to impressed Karen but was insecure as his love interest seemed more infatuated with Natasha then with him.

Edward Dean Mullins was nineteen and the only one from the group that comes from an intact family that goes to church. He is struggling with self-esteem issues, however, as women reject him until he meets Natasha. James Bryant is fourteen but seemingly the most volatile of the "Wild Bunch". His mother has abandoned him and left him alone with an alcoholic father. Natasha and Karen met him on a street corner and picked him up because they thought he looked "cool." Mostly likely, they saw him as someone the could use to do their dirty work.

"I had been friends with Joe for awhile," Natasha said. "Joe was dating Karen. Crystal needed a place to stay and she was friends with Dean (Mullins)."

Jason was the last entry into the "Wild Bunch." It was apparent, however, that he and Natasha didn't always see eye to eye. According to detectives, Jason was not as "controllable" as others in Natasha's group.

"Jason didn't make a huge impact on me," Natasha said. "He seemed dangerous. Like people pretend to be bad. I thought that was his hook. He was the 'bad boy.'"

Natasha's mother's trailer would be their primary hangout where they would drink, do drugs and later plot out their killing spree.

"Prior to leaving (for the road trip)," Bell said. "The defendants would watch 'Natural Born Killers.' That movie depicts individuals who are carefree, killing people. There don't appear to be from that movie, any consequences (to violence). They may have felt that there were not going to be any consequences for their actions. I really don't know what it takes for a group of people to take on that mentality of murder. They had no concept of tomorrow. Or consequences. And they just don't care."

The members of the gang become increasingly excited as they discuss the prospects of what will take place on their killing spree. Finally, they have some excitement in their boring, despondent lives with Natasha at the head.

"She seemed to be the leader of the group," Jones said. "And someone in the group said 'we're going to make headlines.'"

MOTEL SEVEN PIT STOP

The group piled into Risner's mother's car, a compact Chevy Citation. Before they would hit the highway, they rented out room number seven at the Colley Motel in Pikeville. Despite Natasha's apparent disdain for Jason, the young fourteen year old had cut Natasha's initials into his arm that night at the motel. The group then attempted to burn the satanic numbers 666 into the motel carpet with candle wax.

They would then begin their self-mutilation ritual.

"Me and Karen started cutting," Natasha said. "And at first, it was just to cut. Then I wanted to die. I thought eventually if I cut myself so many times I would just bleed out. Mostly it was just me and Karen drinking each others blood. We just didn't do seances."

Crystal maintains that they were not part of a vampire cult or nor did they worship Satan. "We dressed in black and we'd stand out. And we did self-multilation. We were the freaks, the outcasts."

"We were trying to find answers, " Crystal said during in interview with Campus Life. "We all had been to church. It didn't provide answers. We were interested in Wicca, books on witches and spells. We were anarchists."

"They wanted to go to New Orleans," Natasha said. "Because that was the only place I was familiar with. And I said I wouldn't go back down there without some kind of protection."

Natasha was referring to the fact that she claimed to be raped in New Orleans although no charges were filed.

The motel owner, Jim Cochran, said that he rented out the room to Risner and described him as "polite and courteous". Risner, who also wore the Goth black make-up was described by detectives as "lanky and long-haired." A week before their killing spree, Natasha was in a Pikeville grocery store where she led Risner around by a dog chain fastened to a collar around his neck.

The group started a fire in the motel room and they were worried the manager would call the cops.

"Karen had just gotten into trouble," Natasha said. "And she didn't want to go back to juvenile. Jason just got out of juvenile and he didn't want to go back. And I was ready to run away at any given moment so it just kinda came together. We were all going to run away."

The group then vandalized and burglarized other Colley Motel rooms during their stay. They stole a television set and several pairs of work boots.

ROUTE 666

The group of disaffected youth drove to Forty-Acre Field, a remote campground where other teens would hang out. They started a campfire then at some point that night or early in the morning they burglarized two homes in a town called Paintsville. It was there they stole two semi-automatic handguns.

They thought about performing a carjacking as Joe's mother's Chevy Citation kept overheating. Nonetheless, they went onto U.S. Highway 23 south into Virginia.

The group was ticketed for speeding in Gate City, Virginia on April 6th but were allowed to continue on.

"Based on the evidence of what their stated purpose was," Bell said. "The night before they left. They were preparing to leave Pikeville. Go across the country. Robbing and killing people."

The group then drove into a used car lot and tried unsuccessfully to hot wire a vehicle.

They kept driving and an hour later, they stopped at the Interstate Highway 81 rest stop in Greeneville, Tennessee.

"Karen needed to pee," Natasha said.

Tragedy would ensue as the group came upon the Lillelid family at a truck stop in Greeneville,

THE LILLELID FAMILY

Thirty-four year old Norwegian Vidar Lillelid, his twenty-eight year old wife Delfina, their six year old daughter Tabitha and two year old son Peter were having lunch on a park bench.

Vidar, who worked as a hotel bellman, had taken his family to a religious convention in Johnson City. They were on their way home to Nashville. He had been in the USA for ten years. His wife, Delfina was a native of New Jersey but had parents who had immigrated from Honduras. The two had married in 1989 and moved to Knoxville four years earlier from Miami because they wanted a nice place to raise their two children. The two were described as "devoutly faithful" and "humble" by those who knew them.

"The Jehovah's Witnesses were having a convention abut thirty miles north," Jones recalled. "They had been to that convention and they were going home. Jehovah Witnesses are known for being active in trying to recruit new members. They leave pamphlets and that sort of thing. That may have been the worst thing they could have done."

"I think they were doing a little proselytizing there," Bell said. "It was just part of their religion that they go out and try and talk to people. They saw the defendant's unusual appearance. They may have though that they needed some discussion about the Lord."

Vidar and Delfina approached the group and asked if they believed in God. Natasha spoke for the everyone, saying she dd not believe in God, as he had never come to her aid when she prayed as a child.

"The whole scenario just drips with tragic irony," Dixon said. "On one hand, we have the Lillelid family. They are sweet and naïve. They are following the dictates of their church to go out and invite as many members as they can for their church. Then there are these cult members who a diametrically opposed viewpoint. They have their own beliefs. Only theirs are something far more sinister."

KIDNAPPING AT GUNPOINT

According to Natasha, it was Joe who initiated the kidnapping of the family.

"It was when Joe said he wanted to converse with Vidar about his religious beliefs," Natasha said. "That just brought up red flags, because Joe was not a religious man. I tried to convince him (Joe) that we should just leave and get on our own way. Every step that he took, I was there trying to prevent it."

Natasha stated that it was never their intent to rob and kill the Lillelids. She became alarmed with Joe who went back to his car and got his gun. Then after conversing with Jason, Joe pulled the gun out on the Lillelids.

Detectives confirmed that Joe Risner admitted that he was the one that pulled the gun. Natasha remained steadfast in her own statement that she tried to stop Joe.

"He was like 'nothing is gonna happen,'" Natasha said. "'We just need your car.' All I could do was just look at them and apologize."

Vidar immediately offered his keys and wallet, pleading for the killers to not harm his family.

"They put them in their respective cars and took off," Bell said. "They got off the Interstate. Just a few miles down the road."

"I didn't think that the people that I was around could actually do anything bad," Natasha said. "Even Jason. I thought I could stop something."

Detectives found out otherwise, however. During interviews with the other members of the group, they believed that Natasha was the instigator. She was the one that members of the group thought could "draw on demons" and was the driving force behind the robbery.

Joseph Risner forced the family into the Citation. They drove along until they reach a remote area.

"It's a dead end, gravel, one lane road," Jones said. "They go down the end of that road and force the people out of the car."

The family is terrified. Vidar continued to plead for mercy. Young Peter is clinging to his mother's leg, his arms wrapped tight around her waist.

"This group of very strange looking people is surrounding them and laughing," Bell said. "And they see the weapon."

"I can't imagine what that would have been like," Jones said. "To know that your family was in peril like that."

According to Natasha, it was Risner that pulled the gun on the family but now on the deserted road it was Jason Bryant, the fourteen year old, who held the family at gunpoint.

"All of a sudden Jason pulled the gun up," Natasha said. "All I could see was rage on his face. And Joe walked away from it. He was like, 'I can't do that.' And I was like 'Jason, what are you doing? And he just started cussing. 'Get the fuck outta the way! Get the fuck outta the way! Move! Unless you wanna die, move!

"I got in between Jason and the family to where the gun was pointed at me and tried to convince him to not do that. I begged and I pleaded for what seemed like an eternity for him to stop. When I discovered that there was no stopping him, I begged for at least the children to be saved. He told me that if I didn't move, he would shoot me."

"I don't think I would have moved anyway until he promised and swore to me that he would not harm the children. That's when I moved. I didn't think that I could do anything to prevent it if I was dead."

During the testimony, Natasha, Risner and Karen Howell said that Bryant did the shooting. Bryant, however, said that Risner and Edward Dean Mullins fired the shots and later forced him to take the blame.

Gunpowder was found on Mullins, however. The detectives and prosecuting attorney believed that the entire group somehow were involved in the shootings as over seventeen shots were fired.

"If you wanted to be a member of this group," Bell said. "You had to participate in this ritualistic killing."

"I don't know which (of the family) got shot first," Bell said. "But the rest of them are observing their family being shot."

"The indication was that the children were shot last," Jones said. "The little girl had apparently walked around in her mother's blood. The boy even though he was two years old was shot in the head."

"I didn't watch," Natasha claimed. "I sat in the back of the van and just screamed. Please don't hurt them. Please don't hurt them. Please don't hurt them. Jason said 'Stop fucking crying.' He just laughed."

Six year old Tabitha was shot in the head. Peter was being held by his mother as he was shot. Each of the victim was shot in the eye as a 'signature' move.

"The males were shot in the right eye," Bell said. "And the women on the left."

"It was a ritualized killing," Dixon said. "Call it bonding through murder. They would hoop and holler and cheer each other on. "

The group left Risner's mother's car at the scene as it became stuck in the mud. They stole the family's van, the youths took off in the hopes of going to Mexico.

But not before they had dragged the bodies over, lying the four bodies parallel to each other so it appeared like a four-pointed star.

Joe laughed as they drove over the bodies, hearing the crunch of bone under the weight of the van.

THE AFTERMATH

Vidar and Delfina were found dead, tire tracks across their clothing. Tabitha was still alive when found but died en route to the hospital. Two year old Peter was shot in the torso and the eye. Amazingly, the boy survived although he is now blind in one eye and permanently disabled.

"Peter survived," Jones said. "The two year old boy had been shot through the eye with the bullet exiting the side of his head. It didn't kill him. He's disabled by the extent of his injuries. He had difficulty walking and of course, blind in one eye."

The youths showed no remorse after the shooting. People who lived nearby heard gunshots, laughing and shouting as they left the family for dead. The police were called and the Sheriffs discovered the dead bodies of the Lillelid family.

ON THE RUN

"After you witness something that atrocious," Natasha said. "I didn't know what to do."

The group went on the run, altering their plans to go to New Orleans. Instead, they headed to Arizona/Mexico border.

Two days after the shootings, Natasha and her cohorts were arrested by US Customs and Immigration officials in Arizona.

"They had been down into Mexico," Bell said. "And as they were coming back through the computers at the border had not been functioning. So the border could not check on who was coming in and out. But just as that group came back in the computer suddenly started working. And when they put the license tag in the system they got a hit. And they were arrested there in Arizona."

The detectives and defense attorney who dealt with Natasha after the arrest vary widely from her own well-thought versions of what took place that night.

"She was a vampire who worshiped Satan," said an officer who spoke to Natasha after her arrest. "She was on the dark side. Very bitter towards everyone."

Natasha allegedly told her first defense attorney, Eric Conn, that she was 'Satan's Daughter.' The attorney decided to play up that aspect of her defense as he hoped to get her a lenient sentence if she was declared insane.

"After Eric Conn got up in the devil worship and vampirism," Wallen said. "It kept getting worse and worse."

Natasha blames her first lawyer, Conn, for her lackluster defense.

"I don't know why it was me that was picked out of everyone else," Natasha said. "I know he did a lot of damage to me and my case.

"I didn't tell him that I even had any inclination toward that," Natasha recalled. "I knew he was a lawyer wanting to represent me pro bono. At no point had I ever been a satanist. Ever. Once something like that is said. You can't just take it back."

Conn was later replaced by Stacy Street but the damage had been done.

Natasha's current court-appointed attorney stated that "he (Conn) volunteered to represent her, then immediately began negotiating movie rights.

SOUVENIRS OF A KILL

"Each one of these killers," Berkeley said. "Took an individual trophy from their victims. And kept it attached to a chain or a wallet."

Karen Howell took Vidar's social security card and Tabitha's 'Hello Kitty' merchandise. Natasha took Tabitha's social security card and her wallet. Sturgill had taken the keys to the Lillelid home all for souvenirs.

DEATH PENALTY?

"We were very concerned that the proof might focus on the juveniles as being the shooters," Bell said. "Juveniles can't get the death penalty. And if they can't get the death penalty we were concerned that no one else would get the death penalty either. What we reached was an agreement that we'd have a hearing."

A media circus followed the trial as an angry mob descended upon the teenagers as they entered the courtroom.

"Someone yelled that I was Charles Manson's daughter," recalled Sturgill.

In the trial, all six defendants had different stories as to how events took place that night and who pulled the trigger.

"It is my position that it was part of an initiation," Bell said. "That everybody had to participate in the shooting."

"Natasha clearly was the ring leader in all of the killings here," Dixon said. "She was the most articulate and confident of the group. The young men in the group were all shy types, eager from some female validation, with the possible exception of Jason who was a budding psychopath. But again, he was a dim-witted fourteen year old pitted against a smooth-talker in Natasha. Sturgill and Howell looked up to Natasha in their own ways as well. Sturgill was social awkward, overweight. She finally found people she could call friends and would do whatever they said. And Karen would not become violent on her own. These individuals were all like that, they could be violent but needed someone to light the fuse. And Natasha struck the match for everyone.

CONVICTION

Natasha was convicted on March 13th, 1998 with the five other youths. She reached a plea bargain where she plead guilty to all of the charges to avoid the death penalty.

In her court testimony, Natasha maintained that she was not the shooter of the four victims. She kept asserting that she tried to prevent the deaths of the Lillelid family members.

All of the defendants were sentenced to three life terms plus twenty-five years without the possibility of parole.

"She wasn't the shooter," Natasha's mother said, maintaining her daughter's innocence. "She got the same thing as the shooter."

PRISON LIFE

Natasha is housed at a prison in Nashville. She has earned her GED and her mother Madonna claims that her daughter serves as a "mentor to fellow inmates as they work to earn their GED."

"I was a teacher's aide for about a year," Natasha said during a newspaper interview.

Her troubled times continued, however, as on August of 24th 2001, she and death row inmate Christa Pike allegedly attacked a fellow prisoner named Patricia Jones.

They tried to strangle Jones to death with a shoe string after all three were placed in a holding cell with Natasha during a fire alarm.

Pike was on death row for torturing and beating a woman to death when they were Job Corps students in 1995.

Another inmate, the twenty-year old Jennifer Szostecki started the fire which created confusion during the fire alarm. This allowed Christa Pike to gain access to Patricia Jones.

Jones allegedly teased Pike about her upcoming execution.

"All she does is snitch on me and stab me in the back," Pike said during a phone call with her mother.

Natasha allegedly struggled with Jones before Pike came from behind and started to choke Jones with the shoe strings from a hiking boot. Natasha was Pike's friend and Szostecki's "girlfriend."

Letters filed in criminal court show Szostecki's obsession with Natasha.

"I love you," Sozstecki wrote. "I hate you. I miss you. I want you. I need you."

Pike was later charged with attempted murder while there was insufficient evidence to charge Natasha.

"I expected big women with shanks and stuff like that," Natasha said of her time in prison. "You know, like that typical prison scene that you would see in a movie. But it's not like that. You just get up, go to meals, have an hour out for recreational purposes and watch television and read."

PETER LILLELID

Peter Lillelid would be the subject of a custody battle between his USA based relatives and his aunt in Sweden. His aunt and uncle from Sweden won custody and Peter was sent to be in their care.

They kept him shielded from the media and he does not like to read the accounts of what happened to his parents and sister.

A MOTHER'S KILLER :

THE TRUE STORY OF NICOLE KASINSKAS

48

CHRISTINE GOODMAN

Nicole Kasinskas was a quiet, unassuming teenage girl. She was born and raised in Nashua, New Hampshire to Anthony Kasinskas and Jeanne Domenico.

"I lived with both of my parents and my younger brother until I was eleven years old," Nicole said. "And my parents divorced and my Dad moved out."

"I think after my parents got divorced and I was dealing with that, I became a little bit angrier. I had a little bit more resentment towards him, and it did change my perspectives about myself and about life in general, I guess even as an eleven year old."

In May of 2002, she found "romance" as a fifteen year old on-line with eighteen-year old Billy Sullivan.

Sullivan lived in a town called Willmantic where he worked as a line cook at McDonald's.

"Nicole hadn't had a lot of boyfriends," prosecuting attorney Kirsten Wilson said . "She was really caught up by the attention by this guy who was saying amazing things to her about how beautiful she was and what she meant to him."

They would communicate daily through e-mail, letters and phone calls. Despite not having met in person, they both declared love for each other within days, speaking of marriage and planning their future together.

"They filled in sort of the gaps of everyday communication and relationships with fantasies and making these assumptions on who the other person was," Wilson said.

"He lived in Connecticut and so our relationship was almost one hundred percent over the phone," Nicole said. "But it became everything to me very quickly because of the amount of attention that he paid me, and I didn't really feel that I was getting that from anywhere else."

Nicole had been vulnerable to Sullivan's Internet advances as she was a loner with very few friends in high school. She was routinely bullied at school by other girls. On one occasion, she was walking down the hall and one of her bullies had pulled her sweatpants down to her ankles. Nicole was not wearing any underwear, furthering the humiliation. Nicole refused to go back to school the next day after that incident.

"The bullying at school certainly made Nicole vulnerable to someone like Sullivan," forensic psychologist Fiona Russo said. "She's lonely, she's being picked on at school and completely humiliated. She stuck to herself and so when some guy pays attention to her, even when it is only online, her fantasy life goes into overdrive. She's able to project things on him that he doesn't deserve or merit."

The more severe the bullying became, the more Nicole began to withdraw and cling to Sullivan.

"As I got older, it was easier for me to isolate from people," Nicole said. "I think at that point I had just gotten used to being more alone as opposed to being around people. And it just became a part of who I was. Maybe if I was more open or maybe if someone had tried harder to reach out, that it could've been different."

Nicole's mom, Jeanne, was her best friend. Jeanne worked at an elementary school for a period of time, holding down such jobs as a crossing guard, a lunchroom monitor, and a paraprofessional for about three years before taking a job where she worked on group contracts for the Benefits, Brokers and Administration department.

"Jeanne Domenico was well loved in the community," Wilson said. "Hard worker. Really sort of a bright, energetic, sweet woman. She was trying to make her daughter happy."

Despite the bullying at school, Nicole got straight A's at school and made her mother happy whenever she made the honor roll.

"School really became my self-worth and I really identified with, like whatever my grades were," Nicole said. "However I was doing in school I felt it reflected on me personally, because I felt that it was so much a part of who I was. I never got in trouble in middle school. I never got spoken to. I never had a detention. It never really crossed my mind to do anything that would be against the rules."

"It would have been helpful if there was more of an acknowledgment that I was doing so well. I think it also would've been helpful if there was more involvement with guidance or something. Just more of a like a check-in...see how things are going."

"Somehow, someway, Nicole got lost in the cracks," Russo said. "That in no way justifies what she did. It may be how she justified it during this time. Her parents are divorced. She doesn't see her Dad. Her mom is working all the time. There had to have been days where she felt intense loneliness Going to school just to be ignored or bullied. To a fourteen year old girl you really may not see the light at the end of the tunnel. So you seek an outlet. Some turn to drugs. Nicole found her own drug in the form of the words that came out of Sullivan's keyboard."

MOTHER AND DAUGHTER TROUBLES

At least on the surface, there were no problems between mother and daughter.

Until Nicole ventured on-line and met Billy Sullivan.

Her mother found out about the relationship and wanting to make her daughter happy, drove the young teenager out to Connecticut so she could meet Sullivan for the first time.

"This was a two hour drive from Nashua to the place in Connecticut where Sullivan lived," Russo said. "It is easy to say here is where Jeanne made a fatal mistake. But in her mind, it is all innocent. Her daughter is fourteen and begging her to drive out to meet this guy. Begging and begging. Until she finally she relents."

More visits followed but friends and classmates knew little of the teen's relationship. Sullivan had informed some of his friends that he had a girlfriend that was "out of state." Other than that, he revealed very little about his personal life.

"He's quiet, he didn't really like to talk," recalled Danny Goss who was a classmate of Sullivan. "But he was good in school and didn't get in any trouble."

"I think the relationship intensified to a degree that Jeanne herself didn't anticipate," Russo said. "And it is easy to play Monday morning quarterback here but there had to have been some kind of father figure present to say 'hey, this is an eighteen-year old working at McDonald's. You are a fourteen year old honor student. You have a future. Don't blow it on this guy. But it isn't like teens listen to you anyway."

The two teenagers soon discussed the prospect of moving in together. Her mother quickly objected to this idea as well as nixing the idea of Nicole sharing a joint bank account with Sullivan.

But the young man later stayed overnight one weekend with Nicole's mother's full consent.

The relationship is the first for Nicole. She pedestalizes Sullivan as everything she has fantasized about is coming true.

"Nicole had a void in her life," Russo said. "When her parents divorced it certainly affected her psychologically in the way she viewed men. Then along comes Sullivan whose older and more experienced. She gets the love from him that perhaps she sought from her father. The older man, wiser than his years, showering her with attention. She was vulnerable to that."

"Her father didn't have too much to do with her after the divorce. She had that longing in her heart for that male figure. And along came Sullivan."

PERSONAL DEMONS OF HIS OWN

Sullivan, however, had his own personal demons he was fighting.

"He did have mental health issues," Wilson said. "He had been hospitalized a number of times. During high school he had some behavioral issues. Some anxiety, that kind of thing."

It was later revealed that Sullivan had been on numerous psychiatric medications to curb his depression, anger and schizophrenia. He had been weaning himself off the meds, however, and on one occasion he engaged in an argument with Nicole's mother over dinner.

Jeanne had asked Billy if she liked the dinner she had prepared. He said yes and then Jean made the comment that "I bet you don't get that too much at home."

Sullivan was highly defensive over anything that involved his home life. When Jeanne made that comment, he turned hostile.

"Sullivan was protective of his home life," Russo said. "If anyone insulted his mother or if he even perceives that someone is insulting his mother then he gets abusive. He did this to Jeanne, who had obviously made nothing more than an idle comment. That was the first warning sign and the relationship should have ended then and there."

Nicole, however, defended her young beau and from that moment the tug of war for her heart began.

"Nicole's own naivete comes to bore at this point," Russo said. "She has no experience with boys and here is this older guy that she looks up to, almost as a father figure of sorts, who turns her against her own family. Against the one person who loved her the most. Her mother. It is a tug of war that the mother loses simply because her daughter's hormones are raging and she doesn't yet have the emotional capacity to know any better."

After a year of dating, in August of 2003, Sullivan drove out to Nashua to spend a week with Nicole. By this time, they are both fed up with Nicole's mother's objections to their ideas of cohabitation.

"Our relationship was definitely emotionally abusive," Nicole said. "And I think now over time, from looking at it, my perspectives on that have changed so much. I feel like he is responsible for his actions and I am responsible for mine. I didn't really get that and I feel like in order to be emotionally abused, in order to stand for it and stay in it, there's gotta be something missing in you. There's gotta be something hurting already, something is not there, something's not right. And that needs to be figured out, found and fixed. Regardless of how a child is acting or what's coming off, there's more inside that kids need help with or guidance or just to have some type of connection with someone. You need to have relationships with people ahead of time, so that when the bad stuff does happen does happen you don't just come in to it expecting to work it out. Like, you need to have firm foundation with that person in order to work it out."

Nicole continued to side with Sullivan against her mother. The two argued constantly, Sullivan's influence quickly become apparent in Nicole's attitude toward her mother as she found fault with everything she did.

The two teens began discussing an unheard of option.

They began discussing the prospect of killing her mother.

"Well, this is where it starts getting...it's a scary business for me," Nicole said in a jailhouse interview. "I'll tell you that. I feel like I"m gonna cry. I don't talk about this stuff so this is really the first time. I think that my relationship with my mom was good. It was fine. I loved my mom. And...that changed. When...I'm not saying I stopped loving my mom, but...our relationship changed. I'm not gonna say that we were the most open because we weren't. We didn't talk about every little thing. I don't remember ever once talking about my parents' divorce with either of them. But the thing is, we didn't really talk about much of anything. When I was fourteen, I became involved with seventeen year old boy. This is really stemming into why I'm here (in jail) now."

OUT OF CONTROL

"Emotions begin to run high as Sullivan ups the ante in his hatred for Nicole's mother," Russo said. "Nicole is emotionally underdeveloped and has to choose between her mother and her 'man.' It is easy to look at it hindsight but with the teenaged girl's warp logic, she sees Sullivan as her entire world now. So she will do anything for him. Even murder."

Nicole's mom really didn't realize the danger that Sullivan was. She began doing what every mom does, demanding that her daughter stop seeing him, stop chatting with him and concentrate on her schoolwork. Nicole, on the other hand, remained fervent in her desire to move to Connecticut to move in with Sullivan.

"Jeanie, rightfully so, said 'you're fifteen you're finishing school,'" Wilson said. "'You're not moving to Connecticut' and that really upset both Nicole and Billy."

The prospect of not seeing Nicole had an adverse emotional effect on Billy.

"He started talking about killing himself...on the road...driving into a big truck because of leaving me..because of his sadness over it," Nicole recalled. "And I think now it just sounds silly, you know? But it wasn't then, and it was terrifying to me because I didn't...I didn't know how to...because of the way that our relationship was. Because he had become so much a part of my life. I mean, I really didn't feel like I was anything without him. I had nothing in my life at that time...I felt...at that time. So the thought of losing him in that way just wasn't okay with me. And that is unfortunately when conversations started about ultimately what happened. I guess I really I don't really go into too many details but I was sixteen and he was eighteen at that time. And I guess I should give you some background. He killed my mom and I was a part of it. I was not physically there but I knew and I helped him. I was, you know, going through the motions of what was being done. But mentally and emotionally, I don't think I was fully there. I don't think I was fully getting it."

"It was emotional manipulation," Russo said. "It is all so scary romantic for a fifteen year old girl to have some guy who is so in love with her that he is going to kill himself because he can't be with her. She has no one in her life to say 'this guy is a loser nutcase.' There isn't anyone that can talk sense to her. So she falls for the emotional manipulation of a highly disturbed but cunning con man."

Billy had convinced the depressed Nicole that her mother was an obstacle to both hers and his happiness.

"I really just did whatever I could to maintain that relationship because I didn't want to lose that," Nicole said. "I didn't want to lose him. And I quickly learned how it would go if I didn't always do everything that he wanted me to do. At that point...you know, getting to be fifteen...sixteen years old...I would fight more with my mom and there was a lot more to fight about, especially with, you know, this relationship that I was having with this kid."

THE FINAL PLAN

The couple tried different methods to murder Jeanne Domenico.

First they tried to poison Jeanne's coffee. The teens had placed Dimetapp, Benadryl and other drugs into Jeanne's coffee creamer in the refrigerator.

Jeanne used the creamer but didn't die and evidently remained ignorant of the plot on her life. The teens then added bleach to the creamer, wanting to strengthen the amount of poison. It was unclear in a court affidavit if Jeanne ever drank from the spiked creamer again.

The next idea was to set Nicole's mattress on fire with a candle. That idea didn't work because the bedding was made of fire retardant material.

It is unclear how the teens planned to fire up the mattress, whether they sneaked into her Nicole's bedroom and tried to fire up the mattress while she slept.

The third idea was to blow up the fuel oil tank in Jeanne's house. The teens had tied two ropes together which would serve as a wick. Their idea was to set fire to the rope which would then ignite a fire from the fuel tank. This idea was of course unsuccessful.

"These were hair-brained schemes from the start," Russo said, "particularly the fuel tank episode. What is interesting is that these are passive attacks. There is no face to face encounter with the mother, they just really want her gone. But it does show how these were test-runs of sorts. Sullivan was working up his nerve to do something violent. Nicole was building up her psyche. With each unsuccessful dry run, their determination and focus to do the job became greater until finally they realized that physical violence would be the only alternative."

THE ATTACK

The couple decided that Sullivan would do the killing. Nicole waited in the car at a local 7-Eleven where he mother worked part time to make ends meet. She wanted to wait there because she hated her home so much. Her boyfriend obliged, and entered the home of Jeanne Domenico between the hours of six and seven in the evening, waiting for her to come home from work.

The plan was for Billy to kill Jeanne by hitting her on the back of her head with a baseball bat.

Nicole waited anxiously in the car for an extended period of time then began to get worried as to why Sullivan was taking so long.

"Nicole called him and asked him what was taking so long," Wilson said. "Jeanne began getting upset that Nicole wasn't home and kept saying 'where is she? Tell her to come home.'"

Nicole heard her mother's voice on the other end of her cell phone telling her to "come home."

As became her habit, she did not listen to her mother.

"Sullivan did not attack Jeanne immediately," Russo said. "Again, he needed that fuel to add to his fire. So he confronted Jeanne, asking her why they kept refusing them to be together. Jeanne would speak logically like any adult would. She's underage. She's still in school. Of course, none of this would get into the head of Sullivan."

Jeanne made the mistake of turning her back on the young man. He then hit her across the back with the baseball bat.

"It looks as if Jeanne tried to get out of the kitchen door," Wilson said. "Billy started grabbing kitchen knives and attacking Jeanne with the steak knives from the state clock in the kitchen."

The attack was, in a word, brutal.

Sullivan stabbed Jeanne numerous times near her heart and stomach. He stabbed with such ferocity that the blade broke off the knife and he had to retrieve another. Then he stabbed her eight times in the throat.

"A number of the steak knives snapped off during the course of the attack," Wilson said.

According to later testimony by Sullivan, Jeanne managed to get a hold of one of the knives and tried to fight back. At this point, however, she is stunned and bleeding. Sullivan realizes that he is in trouble and goes in to finish the job.

Sullivan stabs her repeatedly as Jeanne tries to get away. A blade enters her lung.

"I'm done," were Jeanne's final words.

He then changed his clothes and cleaned the blood off. He then went back to Nicole, telling her to go inside the house to check for any weapons that he may have left behind. He also told her to get a towel.

The murder complete, Sullivan returned to the vehicle and announced that he had done the deal.

The couple, however, had a deal. It was now time for Nicole to do her part. She would help clean up the evidence left behind.

"The fact that she could go and clean up after Billy had killed her mother," Wilson said. "She had to have hit her mother with the door. And then she had to have stepped over her body to clean up for her boyfriend. That she was able to do that was chilling to do me."

Nicole took a cloth and began clean up her mother's blood from the kitchen floor.

"The fact that a psychopath like Sullivan was able to stab Jeanne to death isn't the most blood curdling aspect of this case," Russo said. "The really scary part is how Nicole was able to go back into that house, see her mother laying in a pool of blood on the kitchen floor, then begin to do her end of the bargain, which was to clean up after her boyfriend. The amount of psychological and emotional disconnect here is chilling."

The two then hid the evidence in the outskirts around town before going to a shopping mall in order for Sullivan to purchase new clothes.

Hours after the killing, Nicole finally began to realize the gravity of what has taken place. She realizes that she and Billy were not going off to "see the world." Her best friend, her mother was gone forever.

Jeanne's body would be discovered by her boyfriend later that evening and he quickly called the police. At around 10:15 p.m., Sergeant William Moore and Detective Shawn Hill saw Sullivan and Nicole approach the crime scene.

"They were cocky enough to think they could outwit the cops," Russo said. "By approaching the crime scene and acting all innocent, not knowing what happened, they thought they would deflect attention away from themselves. It really shows you how dumb these two kids were."

The police then stated the teens would have to be separated for an interview. Nicole protested, stating that Sullivan would not know how to get to the police station. The police informed her that they would take him there themselves.

"This is when things start to go haywire in their heads," Russo said. "Nicole is getting nervous, knowing that they will be questioned separately and face the prospect of not having their stories straight. These two were not exactly forward thinking individuals."

The two waited for the police cruisers to arrive and made conversation with Detective Moore. The detective noted that Sullivan did most all of the talking and admitted that he did not like police officers, stating that he had been charged before with crimes he did not commit.

Moore informed Sullivan that he would be given a "fair shake" in the questioning.

Sullivan, however, kept talking. He informed the detective that he had been shopping for souvenirs with Nicole that day and talked about Jeanne's relationship with Nicole. The detective said that Sullivan paced back and forth and then sat down on the trunk of his car.

Twelve minutes later, Detective Linehan arrived on the scene, making contact with both Nicole and Sullivan. Linehan noticed how nervous and "jumpy" Sullivan was. Linehan told Sullivan to "relax" and then the teen explained that he suffered from anxiety but did not need medication. He told the police that he had "no problem" to come to the station for questioning.

Linehan sat with Sullivan in the back seat of the squad car as they headed back to the station. Both of the teens were having casual conversations with the officers but after being questioned separately, they both admitted their involvement, leading police to the locations where they had disposed of the evidence.

"Both of the teenage lovers wilted under the police interrogations," Russo said. "She immediately ratted out Sullivan as the killer while he did the same to her. There was no loyalty for one another while under the police questioning."

Sullivan would be convicted of first degree murder, sentenced to life without parole.

Sullivan, however, did not let his Lothario ways go to rust in jail. He wrote love letters to a girl named Monique Teal who was then sixteen. This occurred while Sullivan was awaiting trial and later Teal's testimony was used in court.

Teal, using a pen name of Monique Sullivan in her love letters to Sullivan, had agreed to a date to marry the now twenty-year old murderer. Teal's mother, however, found out about the letters and forbade him to call or write.

"He just laughed about it," she said. "He said that no matter what my mom would say or do that nothing could keep us away from each other."

"You see him trying the same techniques on Teal," Russo said. "The immediate declarations of love. The flowery language. The idea of them against the world. In Teal's case, however, her mother put a stop to it."

Sullivan admitted to the Jeanne Domenico killing in one of his letters to her, Teal would reveal, although she didn't read from the letter in court. She said she obeyed Sullivan's demands and threw that letter away.

JAIL LIFE

Nicole Kasinskas would plead guilty to second-degree murder.

"My original sentence was forty years to life," Nicole said. "It is now thirty-seven years and a half to life based on a plea that if I acquired my GED I would get two and a half years off. I don't mark days off on my calendar. I don't do those types of things. This is my life now and I want to live it. I don't want to just look at it as one day down closer to my real life. Like this is my real life. I smile a lot and I live a lot and I'm happy a lot and I just prefer it that way rather than get lost in the sadness of it because you can. And I have. But if I...if I can choose not to...if I can be stronger than than then I want to. And it makes me feel freer. It makes me feel that I have more control of my life."

"Her life as a promising honor roll student at fifteen years old with her mother who loved her very much," Wilson said. "She lost her entire life. And for what?"

"I had no goals. I had no hopes and dreams, you know? You need to have your own hobbies and friends and stuff. Outside the relationship, there needs to be that balance. I just never had that, I never figured that out."

"Maybe if someone had said something like, 'I see you, I see that there's more to you than this and I want to see more of you. I'm here for you. I care about you.' I mean everyone needs help, everyone needs support."

KILLER NURSE :

THE TRUE STORY OF GENENE JONES

64

KORI MAYER

Genene Anne Jones was born on July 13th , 1950 in Texas but was given up for adoption. Her adopted parents had three other children. Two were older and one was younger than Genene.

EARLY LIFE

Her adopted parents were Richard and Gladys Jones. Richard, better known as "Dick", a night club and was a gambler. He was a big spender and generous when he was flush. His club was called the Kit Kat Swim Club, the place had a dance floor with a patio and pool outside. His wife Gladys was the disc jockey at the club and the couple lived an extravagant lifestyle. They had a mansion that looked down on San Antonio, would travel often and they would both have pilot licenses .

At the age of ten, however, Genene's father was arrested for stealing the safe of a customer who had been at Jones' club at the time of the robbery. These charges were later dropped.

It could have been due to intimidation on Dick's part. The man was six feet tall, weighed a solid 240 pounds and was bold. He had an aggressive demeanor when needed and his adopted daughter developed the same traits.

His business soon failed, however. The shady Kit Kat Club soon turned into a family themed restaurant which put Dick further into debt. He then sold off the restaurant and earned a living putting up billboards around San Antonio. Genene would later describe helping her father put up the billboards as one of the happier times of her life.

Still, Genene felt as if she suffered from neglect in the adopted home. The parents had paired off the four kids on the basis of age. Genene had an older brother Wiley and an older sister named Lisa. She had a younger brother named Travis who had a learning disability that she doted on and cared for. Nonetheless, she felt jealous of all the attention that Lisa would receive. Genene referred to herself as the "black sheep" of the family and took out her frustrations on her classmates at school. She worked in the library at John Marshall and was described as "kind of bossy" by the high school librarian as she would berate other student volunteers who weren't doing their jobs up to her standards. Short and chubby, Genene felt unattractive and began to become known for lying and manipulating people.

"Lying was like talking for her," one of her classmates recalled as Genene would often tell people that she was related to Micky Dolenz, the band member of the Monkees, and that she would routinely have phone conversations with him all the time.

Tragedy would strike in her teens, however, when her younger brother Travis died in a freak accident.

He had put together a pipe bomb which exploded in his face, sending metal shards into his head. Genene took the loss hard, arriving at the funeral with a large flower wreath, crying hysterically, then feinting.

"You wonder when Genene's mind got twisted," forensic psychologist Dina Foster said. "It had to have been early on in her development when somehow, someway she got a surge of power when she was care taking for someone particularly a child. This was probably her brother, Travis. Being a caregiver for him made her feel important. She realized that she could be respected and have people look up to her until it became twisted."

A year later, her father died of cancer at the age of 56 which further devastated Genene. She had yet to graduate high school and wanted to get married. Her adopted mother refused as she Genene's choice of mate, a dropout named James "Jimmy" Harvey Delany Jr as nothing but trouble.

The two would marry, however, and live in a guesthouse near the mansion. Jimmy, however, was only interested in cars and drinking. The two would squabble often until Jimmy decided to join the Navy. With her husband away a basic training, Genene would not remain faithful, going after both single and married men. She had an affair with the newlywed husband of a former high school classmate. Then she began to tell people she had been sexually abused as a child. After four years of marriage, Genene divorced Jimmy as she stated that he had been physically abusive toward her.

Genene would threaten divorce but the two would reconcile.

"She experienced abandonment twice," Foster said. "The first go around was when her mother gave her up for adoption. The second go around was when her brothers and father died back to back. She had lost two loved ones to illnesses and one to a tragic accident. She felt helpless and out of control. But unlike most people, Genene went the criminal route in order to assuage the pain. She had to do things to get the power and control back."

CAREER LIFE & DIVORCE

Genene entered Mim's Beauty School and became a beautician, finding work at the Methodist Hospital beauty parlor. She had her first child, Richard, in 1972 while she and Jimmy were stationed in Georgia. They would move back to San Antonio but by that time the marriage was failing. She filed for divorce in Bexar County, eight months after Richard was born and stated that her husband was "a man of violent and ungovernable temper and passion" while also accusing him of "unconscionable brutality and physical cruelty." She won a court order that forbade her husband from going near both her or baby Richard. Two months later, however, the couple had gotten back together and the judge threw out the divorce suit.

"Clearly they had an on and off again relationship," Foster said. "Jimmy was hapless, wanting to do nothing more than race cars and party. So in some aspects Genene had found her soul mate, a man who needed taking care of."

But on June 3rd, 1974, Genene filed for divorce again and the couple would battle in the court system for three more years. She would file suit against Delany for failure to pay child support and in August of 1976 she won a contempt citation against him. In March of 1977, both consented to drop the legal battle and in July 17 of 1977 Genene's second child, Heather, was born. She later admitted that Heather had been conceived out of wedlock when she and Delany had another brief coming to terms.

Genene would then move back in with her adopted mother who helped with the babies as she began her training at San Antonio Independent School District's School of Vocational Nursing. Genene was a mediocre high school student but she excelled in the program, earning high grades. She aced the licensing exam and got a job at Methodist Hospital.

Genene only lasted eight months, however, getting fired when she made decisions about patient care in which she had no authority as well as being rude to patients. Genene would later claim that she was fired for standing up to a doctor who was being rude to a patient.

"She was a compulsive liar when she was a kid," Foster said. "And the lying continued into her adult life as it turned into full blown denial. She was never at fault for anything. It was always someone else, doctors, nurses, her mother, her husband. She never lived in the land of responsibility."

REIGN OF TERROR BEGINS

Genene then found work at Bexar County Hospital (now known as the University Hospital of San Antonio) where she was assigned to the Pediatric ICU.

It is here where the trouble officially began.

Her first patient had a fatal stomach disease called necrotizing enterocolitis and the boy died after surgery. Genene did not handle it well, crying hysterically. "She just went berserk," Cherylyn Pendergraft said, the RN that was orienting Genene during this time. Genene went so far as to move a stool toward the baby's cubicle and just sat there staring at the body.

Pendergraft felt the gesture odd considering that Genene had barely cared for the child.

Nonetheless, Genene saw herself as an equal to the RN's on duty and worked extra hard to acquire more knowledge than an ordinary LVN.

She worked the graveyard shift upon hire then transferred to the swing shift where she worked f3 p.m to 11 p.m while frequently volunteering for overtime and extra shifts.

Genene soon took on a reputation as the "nurse who cried wolf" to the many resident doctors who were training at the hospital. She would issue warnings about a child's worsening condition to the intern. If the intern did nothing she would then go to the resident doctor. If that physician did nothing then she would go higher up the chain of command and wouldn't stop until her recommendations were addressed.

Despite her eagerness to be perceived as on the same level as a registered nurse, Genene would skip continuation classes on the proper use of pharmaceuticals. In her first year, she was written up on eight separate occasions for giving the wrong dosage.

Genene wouldn't let any reprimands stop her, however, as she soon became the ward bully in the cramped quarters of the pediatric ICU. She would intimidate other nurses with her coarse demeanor, making more than a few transfer out of the unit to get away from her.

Her bullying tactics enabled her to make the unit her own, as she was the foul-mouthed Queen of the ward, bragging about her sexual escapades and making inappropriate remarks.

"Here we see the beginnings of tacit approval," Foster said. "No one at the hospital wants to put themselves on the line to stand up against her. It is an environment where everyone is trying to cover their own ass. No one wants to play snitch even when this woman is saying and doing all of these inappropriate things."

Even more disturbing is that Genene would also predict which baby would die.

During "report", a time in which the nurses would describe the conditions of their patients during the shift change handover to the next nurse, Genene would play the role of the Grim Reaper.

"This patient is really bad," she'd say forewarning the nurse, or even predicting death."This patient isn't going to make it."

By 1981, Genene would always demand to be assigned to the sickest patients. She seemed to enjoy the adrenaline rush of the code blues and would grieve when the child expired. Genene would hold the dead bodies and sing to it, making sure she would be the one to take the corpse to the morgue.

"She had a twisted hero complex," Foster said. "She thought of herself as equal to any RN. Most LVNs defer to the registered nurses out of education and experience. But it was quite the opposite with Genene. When the shit hit the fan she would be the first to come to the rescue. The problem was that she created these situations where she could be seen as the hero. Remember she didn't give them enough medication to kill them outright. She gave the babies just enough of a dose so that they would go into cardiac arrest. She wanted to be seen as the savior to the parents of the children she was killing. She wanted to be seen as the hero of the ward. This need was so deep-seated that she was willing to kill to get that need met. That need to be seen as a hero. That need to be seen as the most compassionate of all."

TOO MANY PATIENTS DYING

Co-workers became concerned that a surprising number of patients under the care of Jones were dying.

"The other nurses became concerned," said Vincent J.M. Dimaio, the chief medical examiner at the time. "That there were increased numbers of cardiopulmonary arrests on the ward. All her victims were children. The most innocent of the population. This would not have happened if the cases had been reported to the medical examiner's office."

Unlike most hospitals, Bexar County didn't lock their medications in a cabinet. When it become apparent that children were dying in the unit from non-fatal illnesses, the hospital dragged its feet in an investigation. There was a two-week period where seven children died in the unit. These deaths occurred only when Genene Jones was on duty and the patients were under her care.

"Astonishing," Foster said. "The tacit approval now extended to the cover up of children being murdered. The hospital administrators put their own public relations and jobs above the lives of children. It is a travesty of justice that no one at the hospital was ever punished for this."

Genene had an ally in the department in the form of Dr. James Robotham, however. Known as "JR", a reference to the ruthless businessman from the TV show Dallas, Robotham was an aggressive doctor throughout his tenure in the ICU. He had no problem dressing down nurses or student doctors who were not up to snuff or did not bend to his will. He had no hiring authority in the hospital but took on a vital role throughout the ICU by placing the patient's care onto his shoulders.

Genene saw a kindred spirit in Robotham and the doctor took a liking to her. There was one occasion in which he needed assistance and chose Genene over another nurse.

"She had been validated," Foster said. "She also wanted to be acknowledged for her nursing talents and finally there was someone who came along and anointed her as someone who was worthy."

"Robotham's Pet" as some of the nurses would later call her, would nonetheless display a macabre interest when a child came in with a fatal illness. Genene would make it clear that she wanted to be on hand when death inevitably came.

Genene would enjoy calling the parents to inform them of their child's death, sharing in their grief over the phone.

"She was Jekyll and Hyde," Foster said. "With the nurses and staff she would be coarse, demanding and condescending. But with the parents of the children she turned into the ultimate caregiver. Soft-spoken, compassionate, and joining them in their pain. She would have the parents believing that she was the most caring person on the face of the earth."

Never mind the fact that she would orchestrate the medical emergency of the child.

"That was her way of getting attention," Dimaio said. "She was a 'big person'. She was a 'big person' when she resuscitated children. When she brought them back from death's door. And the rest of her life, she wasn't anything."

THE KILLINGS MOUNT

A six month old baby named Jose Antonio Flores came into the unit with non-fatal symptoms: fever, vomiting and diarrhea. Unfortunately, he came under the care of Genene.

The baby soon suffered a seizure went into cardiac arrest and died.

Genene grabbed the dead baby and ran out of the department with the staff having to track down the crying LVN. The infant was later blood-tested and the results revealed that there had been an overdose of heparin, an anti-coagulant.

No one had ordered that the drug be administered and now the staff became suspicious.

When questioned about the baby's death, Genene resorted to manipulation and blackmail. She told the staff that she took records on every child that had died there and she knew which doctor had killed them.

Finally, one of the doctors informed the hospital administration what he suspected of Genene Jones. He had found a book in her possession about how to inject heparin through the skin without leaving a mark.

The hospital administrators, however, did not want the bad public relations fall out that would result from being a hospital that had a reputation for infant deaths.

"Say that they expected one (death) a week," Dimaio said. "All of a sudden they were getting three or four or five a week. I don't think there was any doubt that they had a good idea of what she (Genene) was doing."

"The amazing thing here is that even after the incident with the Flores' baby, Genene was allowed to continue working on the ward," Foster said.

Another child came into Genene's unit, this time to recover from open heart surgery. The child made progress but during Genene's shift he died.

"They notice that all of them (the deaths) were on the same shift," Dimaio said. "And all of them involved patients being taken care of by Genene Jones."

More doctors complained and a committee was set up to investigate. Head nurse Pat Belko and James Robotham were in charge on the hospital end but an outside team of investigators came in to look at the problem.

This third party team declined to put the blame on Genene as their findings were inconclusive.

COVERING THEIR ASS

Confident of they were in the clear, the hospital reports no abnormal deaths to the county medical examiner. Still, the hospital knew that Genene Jones was responsible for the deaths.

"She was left on the ward even though they knew what was going on," Dimaio said. "Someone said why don't we just fire her? Then they said well she'll just sue us and they'll be a big scandal. There were more interested in saving their reputation and not being sued then in the life and health of these children."

In order to avoid a public relations debacle, the administration decided to replace the LVNs in the unit with registered nurses. They said they were raising the "training bar" for ICU nurses and that LVNs would no longer be needed.

"So when they adopted that policy they let her go from that unit," Dimaio said. "Let go by the way, with an excellent letter of recommendation. Even though they knew what was going on."

Genene had been suspected in the deaths of over 47 other children, the NYT noted that the administration of Bexar County Medical Center and the University of Texas Medical school had shredded over 9,000 pounds of pharmaceutical records, records that were created during the time when Jones worked there.

By doing this, these administrators effectively destroyed any evidence that would be helpful in convicting Genene Jones of more crimes. The hospital stated that the shredding of documents was "routine" and a "coincidence", but the district attorney was able to intervene when, acting on a tip from an informant, he stopped the hospital from destroying an additional 50,000 pounds of pharmaceutical and medical records. The dean of medicine at Bexar was then cited for contempt of court when it was discovered that she withheld hospital reports from the grand jury.

"This is certainly an indictment of the hospital," Foster said. "If over 47 children were murdered, than there would have to be justice. The irony here is that the hospital administrators are not that far off from Genene Jones' mindset. They lie, deny and keep things in secret. All for the sake of control. All for the sake of being perceived that they are something they are not. Genene wanted to be seen as a hero but was really a killer. The hospital wants good pr at all costs, even childcare's lives. They are scum."

THE MURDERS CONTINUE

After her release from the county hospital and with a letter of recommendation in hand, Jones found work at a pediatric physician's clinic in Kerrville, Texas.

"She ended up here in Kerrville after she left San Antonio because of all these unexplained deaths," district attorney Ron Sutton said. "Genene Jones absolutely despises me because I brought down her little self-constructed impact."

The clinic was a start-up to be run by Dr. Kathleen Holland. She only had budget for an LVN and immediately thought of Genene Jones. She had remembered Genene and had been impressed by her take-charge personality and competence.

Holland contacted the human resource office at the hospital and inquired about the availability of Genene. Holland knew about the strange rumors about Genene but was willing to overlook them as she needed someone who could bring passion to their start up.

Holland didn't know how true those weird rumors were..

"She would create these medical emergencies," District Attorney Ron Sutton said. "That only she would know to handle. Then she would look like this supreme nurse when she would take care of the emergencies that she created."

Holland's revelation began with Petti McClellan brought in her young daughter Chelsea. McClellan said that Chelsea had a "bad cold" and went into the exam room with Dr. Holland. Genene then took the young baby out of Chelsea's arms, stating that she was going to "play" with the baby so that she and the doctor could talk.

"She had an irresistible compulsion," Foster said. "Doesn't matter where she is at, a hospital, a clinic, she has that compulsion. She'll see the opportunity to be a create the scenario for herself and she takes it."

"The protocol for the doctor's office would be the nurse, Genene Jones, would take the baby into a separate room just she and the baby, to perform whatever cursory examination; weight, blood pressure, whatever," Sutton said. "But during the time Genene would have these children by themselves all of a sudden they would become like a rag doll. And then she would scream out 'the baby's not breathing.'"

Moments later, Genene would cry out for help, saying that the baby couldn't breathe.

Doctor Holland immediately jumped into action, seeing that the baby had gone into a seizure. The child would be transported to a hospital and her life was spared.

The McClellan's expressed their gratitude toward Holland and Genene. They thought the world of the duo, believing that they saved the life of their child.

Little did they know that Genene had injected the child with succinylcholine.

Genene had used various methods to kill children under her care. She used injections of digoxin, heparin and later succinylcholine to cause a "code blue" in her patients. She would revive them afterward and receive praise. The succinylcholine she used is a paralytic that causes a temporary paralysis of skeleton muscles which can affect a patient's breathing. When she injected small children with this drug, the victim would suffer from cardiac arrest.

Petti would later return to the clinic months later with Chelsea. She had actually called the clinic to make an appointment for her son Cameron but Holland insisted that she bring Chelsea in so that she could "check on her."

"My daughter wasn't sick," Petti would later say.

Holland later disputes the claim that she asked Petti to bring Chelsea in instead of Cameron.

Unfortunately, Petti would bring Chelsea in and witness Genene administer two shots. The second shot would cause Chelsea to go into a seizure and later die.

"Once she began doing it," Foster said. "She couldn't stop. She became fueled by the adrenaline. The rush she got by sticking the syringe into the baby. The rush she got in waiting for the child to go into cardiac arrest. The the rush she got by watching the child die and comforting it in its death. She even got off on informing the parents of the baby's death. That is how twisted her mind was."

"Her original intent may not have been to kill," Foster said. "She was all about being seen as the hero, the Superwoman who came into save the day. Why she would target the same child coming in for another routine check-up really shows that she was getting careless about her victims. She had gotten away with it for so long that she didn't care. Plus, the compulsion would override whatever logic and forward thinking she had."

Chelsea's death was initially seen as sudden infant death syndrome.

"That's when we talked to the anesthesiologist," Sutton said. "He said that this child looks like it was coming out from the effects of succinylcholine, and we launched our investigation at that point."

"Soon as she got that first shot," Petti McClellan said, "Chelsey immediately starting reacting to it. And I asked her right off the bat, 'what did you do? What did you do? Something's wrong with her.'".

Genene visited Chelsey's grave and seemed genuinely remorseful.

"She was a psychopath with conflicted emotions," Foster said. "On one hand she had this need to kill and be in control of what others thought of her, specifically as a hero. And the other hand, she may have felt remorse when her 'heroic' efforts didn't produce the results she wanted."

Chelsey's mother, Petti, however, was shocked to see Genene at her daughter's grave.

Holland would later find puncture marks in a bottle of succinylcholine in a storage cabinet that only she and Genene had access to. "There were two holes in the lid of this bottle," Sutton said. "One where she had withdrawn and then she attempted to replace it with saline solution."

With the investigators closing in, Genene began to panic. She arrived at the clinic after lunch and complained to Holland that she was feeling ill...She had overdosed on her anti-depressants and began looking lethargic.

Holland immediately called the paramedics and Genene's stomach was pumped. Later upon her release, Texas Ranger Joe Davis interrogated her about the holes in the bottle of succinylcholine. Genene denied involvement, stating that she would be willing take a polygraph test.

The next day, Holland was shocked to see Genene report for work as if nothing had happened. She then informed Genene that her services would no longer be needed. Genene grew enraged and challenged Holland to take a polygraph. She then stormed out of the office.

Genene would later call back to the office and informed Holland's secretary that she had left a letter for the physician in her drawer.

The letter was a one page suicide note that she had written before she had taken the overdose of anti-depressants.

"There isn't anyway to explain to you why things are going to change. Sometimes, as wrong as it may seem, you have to except what life dishes out.

When your older, and I know your tired of hearing that, but you will be able to understand why, why I have to go away. It doesn't mean I don't love you. Please believe that. No amount of money or worldly goods could every buy my love. It is so deep & strong, it will last for all eternity.

Please explain if you can to Heather & Michael how much I love them. It's such a strong love, I can't put it on paper. I know I'm asking a lot, but I really feel your the only one who could do it.

I'm not guilty of murder, & I hope you believe that. But Daddy's way is right. It takes all the pressure off you and the seven people whose life I have altered.

No one can hurt me with my Daddy. He'll straighten this whole thing out & then we'll go home & everything will be alright. No more problems for you, no more nightmares for me.

Please make sure Michael and Heather are not separated. I know how my mother feels about Heather, but I also know how she feels about Michael. If Debbie or you can't take them together, please be sure whoever does are good people. People with lots of love.

Please don't be angry. I'm going with Daddy because I miss him and I want to be with him. He'll take care of both of us.

You'll be fine. Please believe that.

I love you,

Genene

Genene had attempted to frame Holland for the murders but all evidence pointed to her. All said and done, Genene had poisoned at least six children at the clinic. Three of the parents continued to utilize Holland as their pediatrician while three other families sued both Holland and Genene Jones as they believed that Holland knew or should have known about Genene's murderous ways.

The criminal investigation began and Chelsea's body was exhumed, revealing traces of the succinylcholine.

Her exact numbers of victims remain unknown as hospital officials first "misplaced" then destroyed records of her activities to prevent lawsuits after Genene's first conviction.

Genene would go on trial on January 15th, 1984 for the murder of Chelsea and injury to the other children. On February, 15, 1984, Genene was convicted of murder after a three hour deliberation. She was given the maximum sentence of ninety-nine years. In October, she went on trail for injuring Rolando Jones with an injection of heparin. She was sentenced a total of 159 years with the possibility of parole that came up after serving ten years.

In 1985, Gene was sentenced to 99 years in prison for killing fifteen month old Chelsea McClellan.

Later that year, she was sentenced to a term of sixty years in prison for the attempted murder of Rolando Jones with heparin.

"I've had several cases that stand out in my mind," Sutton said. "But this one is particularly heinous because of death to small children.

SERIAL KILLER TO BE RELEASED

Genene Jones is now set to go free because of a legal loophole in the form of She is now scheduled for mandatory release in February 2018 due to a Texas law that prevents prison overcrowding. Genene has been a prisoner who has exhibited "good behavior", becoming eligible for the release.

"Please, please, please, do not let this person walk," Petti McClellan said.

"Genene Jones is probably one of the worst types of serial killers because keep in mind who her victims were," said Andy Kahan, a victim advocate. "Defenseless, voiceless, babies. One of the nation's most diabolical serial killers in our country's history is set to be legally released,"

"I was so angry that it went on for so long," Cherlyn Pendergraft said. "That so many children had to die."

Jones now claims to be sickly and is housed in medical jail unit.

"Am I prepared that she walks?" McClellan asked. "No. Because she's gonna hurt another child. I don't want to hear that she's sick. Or that she's old, she's two years older than I am."

"There is absolutely no reason for Genene Jones to be walking the streets," Foster said. "She has a compulsion that has to be satiated. She needs to be locked up for the rest of her life."

The current District Attorney is looking to re-open old cases against Jones in order to keep her in prison.

LESBIAN VAMPIRE KILLER:

THE TRUE STORY OF TRACEY WIGGINTON

82

TRISH SAMUELSON

The mutilated body of 47-year old Brisbane council worker Edward Baldock was found on the morning of October 22nd, 1989 in Kangaroo Park. He was naked, stabbed multiple times and had his throat slashed so severely he was nearly decapitated.

The perpetrator was a woman named Tracey Wigginton, a violent lesbian who reportedly drank her victim's blood after she had severed his throat.

The killing was dubbed the Lesbian Vampire Murder and it sent shock waves through the entire country of Australia.

EARLY LIFE

Tracey Wigginton was born in 1965 and raised in a small northern coastal city called Rockhampton. Her mother had been adopted early on, raised by an affluent couple by the names of George and Avril Wigginton. The Wiggintons had two other adopted daughters, Dorrell and later Michelle.

Avril would brutalize the young girls, abusing them without mercy. She would often whip them with electrical cords and a chained hose.

She also hated men.

"When you grow up, men will do horrible things to you," Avril would warn her young adopted daughters. "All they want is sex."

She would save all of her affection and love for her pet chihuahua which she carried around like a baby.

The girls would remain indoors for the most part while under the care of the Wiggintons. Rhonda, however, would leave home in 1965 to marry Bill Rossborough and give birth to her daughter Tracey.

The man would prove to be a drifter and leave Rhonda less than a year after they were married. Rhonda would be forced back to live in the home of her adopted parents.

She then met a man from out of town and decided to live with him. Rhonda left Tracey in the care of her own adopted parents while she was only four years old and three years later the Wiggintons formally adopted the young Tracey.

GOLDEN CHILD OR BLACK SHEEP?

Unlike her mother and the other adopted siblings in the home, Tracey would be spoiled by her grandparents. She had another sister during this time, a girl named Michelle who was older and half-Indian.

While the grandparents doted on Tracey, Michelle would be the subject of routine beatings. Avril would whip her and once locked her in a dog kennel overnight.

This abuse troubled Tracey greatly as she had formed a bond with her adopted sister. Avril would do everything to keep the two from becoming close, often telling Tracey that Michelle was a "bad influence" and that Tracey was not allowed to play with her.

Later, Michelle was blamed for something Tracey did and ran away from the Wigginton home at the age of sixteen.

Tracey has stated publicly that she "loved her grandfather dearly" but also claimed that he started to demand sex with her after she turned eight (she had informed a fellow classmate about the abuse at the age of ten.)

SCHOOL TROUBLE

The Wiggintons paid for Tracey to have private schooling. She learned art, music and dance. Her troubles started to mount in junior high, however, when she was expelled for allegedly "molesting other girls."

"Her childhood was in a word, horrid," forensic psychologist Gary Harding said. "There were unsubstantiated rumor that her father abused her. What is certain is that Tracey had been abandoned by her mother and was subject to the constant misandry of her adopted grandmother. Avril hated men and certainly passed that down to Wigginton. The incidents of molesting other students could be an indication of her repeating her own abuse, certainly. Because of her size, she would always have been one of the biggest students in the class and certainly the biggest girl. She may have been acting out to gain power and experimenting with her sexuality."

Students were afraid of her as one student commented "I'd always stay clear of her – she had that strange evil look."

Tracey was then sent to a Catholic convent school (Range Catholic School) but wound up dropping out of the institution.

She had grown to be a large young woman, 5'10" and weighing over 240 lbs. During her trial, one news reporter described her as having a "huge buttocks and thighs."

"The physical transformation was simply astonishing," Harding said. "It is no exaggeration to say that Tracey looked like a super sweet and cute kid. Long hair, earrings and long dresses. You compare and contrast her childhood photos to the woman she became and it brings a tear to your eye."

DEATH AND INHERITANCE

Wigginton's adopted parents would die within two years of one another, leaving her devastated.

Abandoned by those closest around her through death or choice, Wigginton would carry around a security blanket with her throughout the rest of her life. This would come in the form of an old pillowcase she called her "bi-lo." She would twirl the material around her hands and caress her face with it. When she didn't know the whereabouts of "bi-lo" she would become hysterical and search around frantically for her security blanket. Sometimes she would wear it under her clothes, around her neck like a scar and place it under her pillow when she slept.

"Of course the security blanket screams abandonment issues," Harding said. "She needs a constant in her life. Something she could count on to always be the 'same', so to speak. So that pillow case became her security but unlike most children who utilize such a psychological tool, she never grew out of it."

Tracey would receive a sizable inheritance, getting an initial payment of $75,000 which she blew through on clothes and a motorcycle. After the death of her parents, she went over to her aunt Dorrell's house and painted the walls with swastikas and obscenities.

PERSONALITY TRANSFORMATION

Wigginton's look would slowly change from a sweet-faced, long haired girl who had numerous boyfriends to an intimidating "butch" obsessed with the occult.

Her roommate was the first to notice the change in Wigginton. A gifted artist, Tracey would often draw roses and other flowers in bright, happy depictions. As time went on, however, her art became darker. She started creating "frightening, mythical monsters" while drawing pentagrams constantly with different demons and gargoyles around them. She would eventually carve a pentagram into the back of her hand with a knife.

Her physical transformation was gradual as she would cut her hair shorter and shorter until she had a full military buzz cut. She stopped wearing anything feminine like dresses and heels, instead electing to wearing masculine looking jeans and tops.

Wigginton adopted an all black look, with leather jacket and calf length boots.

In her left boot, she carried a knife.

"Physically the butch in Tracey was beginning to appear," Gagliardi wrote in Lust for Blood. "Short, spiky hair hair, predominantly black outfits, studded leather. On one occasion she returned to Range College in an army uniform offering 'to smarten the kids up.'"

Her interest in the occult became all too apparent as she would wear a circular silver belt buckle with a five-pointed star inside. The tattoos on her body included a black rose on her right upper arm, a large Merlin on her left upper arm, the Eye of Horus on her left hand and another knife-etched pentagram on her right hand.

She purchased a motorcycle from her inheritance and squandered the rest on booze and bar hopping. Wigginton soon became known in lesbian circles as "Bobby" or as some described her as the "big butch bitch from up on the hill."

"It isn't uncommon for people to rename themselves when they want an identity change," Harding said. "In Wigginton's case, however, it may have been a case of multiple personality disorder. Her 'Bobby' persona may have gotten so strong that it overtook other aspects of her personality. The 'Bobby' persona is what gave her power and strength while 'Little Tracey' was helpless, useless and abandoned."

LEAVING SCHOOL

Wigginton would drop out of school at the age of seventeen in 1982. She would have a dust-up with her biological mother, punching her in the face. She then met a bisexual woman in a bar named "Sunshine". Sunshine was the opposite of Wigginton, petite, blonde and with the ability to draw attention from men and lesbians alike. The two began dating but Sunshine would often cheat on Tracey with other men, leaving Wigginton hurt and humiliated. Despite the cheating, Wigginton would press Sunshine for marriage and the two would exchange vows in a ceremony conducted by a Hare Krishna.

Four years later, she would inherit another $75,000 from her adoptive parents estate.

Tracey burned through the cash quickly as she moved to a seaside resort town called Cairns. Needing money, she found work as a bouncer in a gay nightclub.

She briefly returned to school, starting a course in hospitality but it wasn't long before she dropped out. Her "marriage" to Sunshine fizzled as the blonde woman left her for another man. Devastated, she asked the owner of the club where she worked to impregnate her. They would have intercourse in front of a group of "six close friends" and Tracey would become pregnant but lose the baby in a miscarriage.

"There really isn't any surprise that Tracey would burn through the $75,000," Harding said. "What is surprising however is the fact that she would adopt such a submissive role to Sunshine. Playing the part of the dutiful man, it sounds like the woman's bisexuality didn't sit too well with Wigginton. She would spend long hours sleeping in a fetal position after the two would fight or she would find out that Sunshine was with a man."

ASSEMBLING THE TEAM

Wigginton remained fascinated by the black arts. She held seances, read tarot cards and was eventually able to surround herself with a group of lesbian friends who had similar interests.

"Tracey was one of those people who took diametrical opposition to her own upbringing," Australian forensic psychologist Gary Harding said. "She wanted to rebel against her family, her grandmother, mother and their Catholicism. She thought it better to embrace the exact opposite of the religion of the family of her choice, the dark arts if you will. It is a form of defiance, a form of control. The older she got the more she wanted control so the more she got involved in the occult. When she did this, she was able to attract a group of young women who felt the same way."

"Tracy Wigginton had a personality to match her 17 stone (240 lbs) frame – big," wrote Gagliardi in Lust for Blood. "She died her hair midnight blue and tattooed her body. She was deeply committed to all her causes: lesbianism, occultism and devil-worship. Before long she had coerced her friends from the Valley to kill for her."

Wigginton assembled a group of lesbian friends which included Lisa Ptaschinski, Kim Jervis, and Tracey Waugh. All three of the women fell for the charm of Wigginton who dazzled them with her stories and knowledge of the occult.

Part of the reason Wigginton was able to get these women under her spell was through intimidation. She had convinced her girlfriend Lisa that she had the "ability to disappear except for her eyes."

"Wigginton was a devil worshiper who could disappear," Waugh said, dovetailing Lisa's sentiment. "Leaving only her 'cat's eyes' visible."

The women all dressed alike, wearing black leather outfits and black t-shirts. They would meet in graveyards and drink, holding seances.

During one meeting, Wigginton instructed them that she needed "fresh blood" and that they need to find her a victim.

"Wigginton loved holding court," Harding said. "Not only was her physique much larger than the rest of the young women, her personality was as well. She liked going on rants about the devil and her own vampirism. The other girls were in awe of her."

"Tracey Wigginton was the main instigator," criminal attorney Adrian Gundelach said. "She was telling these girls and leading them on the path to believe that she was a vampire. And that she needed human blood to keep going."

"There was a lot of buzz in the media about all of the women being lesbians," Harding said. "Remember this murder took place in the late 1980s so there was still a lot of judgment and taboo surrounding this sexual preference. Lesbianism was thought of as an aberrant behavior and Wigginton looked to play the stereotypical role of the violent butch who sought to dominate their partners rather than give pleasure."

"Initially, the media reported that Baldock was the victim of a group of man-hating, devil worshiping lesbians. They described Wigginton as being this beast, which she was, but the fact that she was both a lesbian and a vampire gave the story a lurid feel, and the media took full advantage."

A FULL-FLEDGED VAMPIRE

During interviews with police, Kim Jervis would state that Wigginton had captured bats and kept the creatures in her house. Remaining true to all of the vampire legends, Wigginton avoided mirrors and didn't have any in her residence. She avoided sunlight, preferring only to come out at night.

Wigginton would tell her friends that she needed blood to survive and could not eat solid food. She would go to the grocery store and obtain pig's blood which she drank daily for sustenance.

Jervis had taken a drive with Wigginton the Monday before the day they planned to do the killing. Wigginton had rambled on about Satanism and the devil worshiping hierarchy. She informed Jervis that Satan wanted her to be a "destroyer." Then getting all the women together, Wigginton got them all to agree that would find a random victim so that she could "feed."

"(Tracey) was like a shark in a feeding frenzy," Lisa Ptaschinski would say later. "Because of her cravings for blood.

Jervis would say later that she thought the plan was a "joke" but she brought a knife during the drive to find a victim.

What wasn't a joke was that Wigginton would drink the blood of the women in her circle of "vampires".

"I just can't understand how three other woman would follow this other woman with horrific ideas," Gundelach said.

"I said have you seen her drink the blood?" Detective Pat Glancy would ask one of the women during their interrogation. "She said 'I have given her blood. I use my blade that I use for leather work and I slit my veins for her and she sucked the blood from my veins.'"

Wigginton would prefer the blood of Lisa Ptaschinski, drinking her blood but not becoming ill.

"That's a head scratcher," Harding said. "If you drink blood, human blood, you're going to get sick. At a minimum, you're going to be sick to your stomach, literally and figuratively. But this was part of their rebellion. Also remember that vampirism has been noted in psychiatric journals. There are certain people who mistakenly believe that they have this 'need to feed' as Tracey put it. It is a mental sickness. Obviously, a red flag that you're dealing with a psychotic individual. Why these women went along with the program is a indictment on their intelligence."

FINDING THE RIGHT MAN

"They planned to get a man," Detective Pat Glancy said. "That man that they got was poor Mister Baldock I'm afraid."

Two nights after Wigginton declared that she needed to find a "fresh victim", the women gathered up nights and piled into their car, like vampires on a night hunt.

They girls cruised around and found Baldock by sheer choice. He presented a vulnerable target, middle aged with a pot belly and stone cold drunk.

The four women pulled up in their car alongside him, aggressively flirting.

Baldock was feeling lucky as he had just won a dart game over his buddies at a nearby pub. He was a normal average Joe, forty-seven years old with a wife and kids waiting for him at home.

"He was very inebriated when he left (the bar)," Gundelach said. "He had a blood alcohol of .3 percent. So he's an easy victim to lure into the car with four young girls."

Baldock entered the vehicle as the women offered him a lift. Wigginton more than hinted that the girls would provide sex for him.

"There's obviously talk that she's (Tracey) prepared to have sex with him," Gundelach said. "That she'd give him a good time. I think she also indicated that the other girls were available if he felt like them."

The young women drove Baldock down to the secluded banks of the Brisbane river. Wigginton led him out of the car and the two walked to an old boat shed off the water.

"The three waited in the car while Baldock was led down the back (of the shed)," Glancy said.

Wigginton had no qualms in her mind that she would kill Baldock. But she made out with him and got the man to take off his clothes.

She stopped right before penetration, however, and told Baldock that she needed to get something from the car.

Baldock, although drunk, still had his guard up and shoved his wallet under the door of the boat shed so he can get it later.

"He had that sixth sense, I suppose," Gundelach said. "He thought he might be robbed. So he slipped his wallet under the corrugated door under the nearby sign."

Baldock found a loose credit card on the ground. He assumed that it belonged to him as he slipped that under the door with his wallet as well.

"The fact that Wigginton dropped her credit card is a miracle," Harding said. "Psychiatrists thought, and I agree, that somehow, someway that other facet of Tracey's personality came out. That side of her that still had a modicum of right and wrong, the 'Big Tracey' beat out 'Bobby' for just a brief moment. Just long enough to drop the card. A way to self-sabotage her own evil efforts. I shudder to think what would have happened if she didn't drop the credit card. The authorities would have looked for a man or a gang of men. Wigginton and her followers just didn't fit the profile and we would have been left with another unsolved mystery. And they most likely would have gone on to kill again."

Wigginton got back to the vehicle and told the women that she was going to kill Baldock. She got her knife and asked for them to join her.

Only Lisa followed her out as Waugh and Jervis stayed in the car. When Lisa and Wigginton came upon Baldock again, the idea was that they both were going to attack him.

Lisa, however, backed out.

Wigginton didn't.

"I walked around him," Wigginton said. "I took my knife out of my back pocket. He asked me what I was doing. I said nothing and stabbed him...I withdrew the knife and stabbed him on the side of the neck. I stabbed him on the other side of the neck and I continuously stabbed him. I then grabbed him by the hair...and pulled him back, stabbing him in the front of the throat and, at that stage, he was still alive...I stabbed in the back of the neck again, trying to get into the bones, I presume, and cut the nerves. I then sat in front of the tilt-a-doors and watched him die."

Wigginton then ordered Lisa to go back to the car and wait as she drank the man's blood.

Drinking as much as she could, Wigginton then washed up in the river and returned back to the vehicle. The women asked if she had "fed" and she said yes.

Wigginton would never admit blood drinking aspect of the crime to the police.

Her cohorts, however, would be adamant that she drank Baldock's blood. Waugh claimed she smelled blood on Wigginton's breath as they drove back to Jervis' place.

"She looked almost satisfied" Jervis recalled. "Like a person would look if they had just sat down to a three-course diner-which is a gross thing to say."

ONE WOMAN'S BRUTALITY

The sheer violence of the attack left even the most hardened Australian police in shock.

"Tracey stabbed him as hard as she could," Glancy said. "The knife went right to the hilt. She said she got the knife and tried to get into the bones. That was her words. Try to get into the bones."

Wigginton's first stab was into Baldock's back. She nearly severed his spinal cord.

"She stabbed him seventeen or eighteen times according to the pathologist," Gundelach said. "The hole in his back was the largest."

She sliced his throat and then began sucking his blood.

"It was a very depraved and very cruel murder," Gundelach said. "And it's one of the worst."

"When I rolled the body over," said Detective Pat Glancy. "I truly thought the head would detach from the body. It was most uncomfortable."

The young women thought they had gotten away with the murder. The killing was random and there were no witness. But they left behind a clue (the credit) that would have them in custody within hours.

"I don't think we even considered the idea of it (the perpetrator) being female," Glancy said. "We just assumed that it had been done by a man or a number of men."

"It was hard to believe the allegations or the report was true," Gundelach said. "As it turned out everything was true."

"For a short while, at least, Wigginton was able to live out her fantasy," Harding said. "She had visualized that scene of chopping up a man for so long it must have seemed like old hat. That is probably why she was able to go through with a heinous act without the aid of drugs or stimulants like so many other killers. She had built up to this point with her devil worship and wannabe vampire ideas. She become immersed in the darkness so much that everything culminated in that night. She didn't hesitate while the other girls did."

"The irony of her actions is probably lost on her. She spent her whole life rebelling against the church that she was raised in yet the Bible verse 'As a man thinketh, so is he,' is a fitting prophecy of her own life. She thought about darkness everyday, immersed herself in evil and eventually become the embodiment of what she trained herself up to be."

VAMPIRES AND THE MEDIA

The media focused almost exclusively on the vampiric element of the case. Wigginton and the others looked the part with their Gothic clothing and stark, masculine looks.

"She (Tracey) fell in love with the idea of being a vampire," Harding said. "Just like in the movies, the vampire chooses a victim at random. Follows him. Seduces him. And the way they (the young women) dressed like these Goth chicks out for a good time, plenty of cleavage and what have you. Then they killed him and drank his blood. This was all heavily influenced by vampire culture, movies and books. It was all a part of their little fantasy world that they made come to life in the form of killing Baldock."

Furthermore, the media focused a great deal on the lesbian aspect of the murders. Feminists were up in arms as they felt lesbians were being castigated.

"Tracey Wigginton was the dominant in the dating relationships," Harding said. "Lisa was her submissive although it has been said that she was dating Waugh. So there are these open relationships going on and the lurid stories that go along with that. What was lost was that a family man lost his life that night."

A VAMPIRE THAT WILTS UNDER PRESSURE

The four women got together and had an agreed upon story that they didn't see or do anything. Wigginton was arrested within hours of the discovery of the credit card as was Kim Jervis.

Wigginton said that she and Jervis had been at the park during the day and that she recalled seeing a suspicious-looking couple milling around the area. When told that Jervis gave a different story, Wigginton began to wilt. She said that they had, in fact, been at the park at night but they tripped over a body in the dark.

"I had been too frightened to report it to the police," she said after being told that Jervis told the police that they had discovered the dead body at night.

"We walked behind the sailing club," Tracey said. "There we saw the body...it just looked terrible...he had blood all over his face. We just had to get the hell out of there."

Lisa Ptaschinski knew that her friends were being interrogated. She left her home an emotional mess, not knowing whether she should run and hide or just wait.

In the end, she could not bear the anxiety.

She turned herself in at the Ipswitch police station and gave them all the gory details.

Later, Kim Jervis and Tracey Waugh would enter the police station and give their statements on what took place.

SPLIT PERSONALITY?

"She (Tracey) had her story already made up and only admitted things she knew we knew," Glancy said. "It did not worry us but she could unnerve weaker people; a typical psychopathic personality.

Detective Sgt Glenn Burton had a brief but an uncomfortable meeting with Wigginton. He poo-poohed the idea that she had hypnotic powers but he was "impressed with the strength of her personality, a voice which-using two or three words at a time...When she looked at you it was almost as if you didn't exist. It was a stare that went through you."

Prior to the trial, Wigginton was forced to undergo twenty-six hours of hypnosis. She was examined by a couple of different psychologists and psychiatrists who determined that the woman suffered from a multiple personality disorder. It was revealed that she had four different personalities.

Bobby: contemptuous, callous and cynical, the murderous side of her personality.

Big Tracey: anxious and depressed, distressed by the murder, a good personality believed by psychiatrists to have left Wigginton's credit card at the scene of the crime.

Young or Little Tracey: childlike and naïve, who presented Wigginton's childhood days.

The Observer: calm, detached and rational, who acted as a record of the thoughts and actions of Wigginton's other personalities.

They also believe that there was a fifth personality named Avril who was a nightmarish presence that controlled Bobby by "screaming in her head."

All of the four women were brought to trial although none of them took the stand. Videotaped interviews were brought forth instead which revealed the extent of Wigginton's power over the young women in her "coven."

"Tracey has mind power," Waugh said in her interview. "She has a hold on you. She is like a magnet. You can't stop yourself from doing what she tells you to do."

Waugh would become the only defendant acquitted by the jury. Her own attorney described her as a "coward who was vulnerable to Wigginton's manipulations." He also emphasized that Waugh had in fact been Tracey's "reserve victim", that she would be killed in the event that blood could not be found elsewhere.

"Waugh, the most attractive of the three sat demurely with her wide brown eyes downcast," wrote Garibaldi. "Looking the picture of innocence, she prompted the prosecutor to remark that she looked "like a 16 year old schoolgirl."

Jervis' attorney, on the other hand, tried a different tactic. She was described as a "young lady of good character who collects dolls and Garfield cats."

He emphasized the fact that he believed that she was "sucked in" by Wigginton, stating "Wigginton wrote the script, Wigginton wrote the story and she conscripted an extra, my client. Wigginton gave Kim Jervis the chance to step from the audience on to the stage so she could take part in it."

Jervis, however, was found guilty and sentenced to eighteen years despite the fact that she was not on hand for the murder. She had waited in the car with Waugh throughout the killing.

Lisa Ptaschinski, meanwhile, was characterized as an emotional unstable woman who had no idea of the consequences of her actions. Lisa really thought Tracey was a vampire and was a "willing victim" to please Tracey.

"She had a strong attraction," Lisa said. "I don't know what, it's normally very unusual for anyone to push me around. She dominated me more than anyone has in my life."

SENTENCING

In 1991, Wigginton was sentenced to life in prison by the Supreme Court of Queensland with a minimum of 13 years.

Her mother, Rhonda Hopkins, remained angry at the way her daughter was portrayed in the media.

"All I want to get across to people is that she (Wigginton) is not an evil person at all," Hopkins said. "She is not a vampire and she did not drink blood...Tracey is a murderer but she is still a person and she still has rights...It would do a lot to restore Tracey's faith in human nature if she saw the truth printed."

"I remember one time when we had a sick chook and someone told Tracey to chop its head off and put it out of its misery, she couldn't do it. She did not drink blood."

Things did not get much better for Wigginton. In 2006, she attacked another inmate and a prison guard. She lapsed into a depression but found work as the prison librarian.

In 2008, it was rumored that Lisa would be set free from prison after nearly 22 years. Lisa would be released under the resettlement leave program, where she would be given a maximum of 12 hours leave every two months for six months. These reports were later shown to be false.

Jervis would be found guilty of manslaughter and sentenced to 18 years. Her sentence was later reduced to twelve years on appeal.

Waugh would be acquitted of being an accessory.

RELEASE

In her one and only interview, Wigginton expressed remorse for her actions and stated that she has "terrible dreams of his killing."

She stated that she had no connection with Satanism and was herself frightened by the variety of exorcists who met with her at the jail to "rescue her from the devil."

"I was off the planet when I killed," Wigginton said. "I wasn't even my usual doormat self-I was an animal."

She described her killing as a "metaphorical revenge against all those who had hurt her."

"Once I had started (stabbing) I couldn't stop," Wigginton said. "I couldn't see Mr Baldock-I kept seeing my grandmother, my grandfather, my mother, my father and all the people in my life who had hurt me."

Wigginton made numerous unsuccessful parole applications until 2011 when the parole board set her free on January 11th 2012. Her attorney, Josh Fenton, successfully lobbied for her parole as he stated that Wigginton was in such poor health that it was impossible for her to harm anyone once she was released.

He stated that Wigginton suffered from a chronic and debilitating back condition and a knee injury that required crutches for her to walk.

"I don't think she should be released," Glancy said. "I really don't. It was just a vicious crime and done by a woman, a very, very cold calculating woman."

"Murder is a terrifying experience," Wigginton said. "It's extremely scary to have that much power. It's playing God with life and death. Nobody should have that sort of power...but we all do."

PIN UP QUEEN KILLER :

THE TRUE STORY OF SAMANTHA SCOTT

DALE CROWELL

Andrea Claire aka Samantha Scott had was born in 1941 and grew up in New Jersey.

At the age of 15, Andrea claimed that her mother forced her to marry the man who got her pregnant. In Andrea's words, she was rape but according to her mother, the 22-year old man got Andrea drunk and "took advantage." The man was a friend of her sister and reportedly was either set up on a date with her or picked her up from basketball practice.

Known to her friends as "Drea," Andrea would divorce the man after over two volatile years of abuse but the union still produced two children. Armed with only a 9th grade education, Andrea had no skill set and bounced from job to job. She began working as secretary, waitress, escrow worker, model and touring exotic dancer.

CAROUSEL OF MEN

She married again in a union that lasted three days as her new husband didn't want her to bring her children into the marriage (she met him while setting a trap to find out who was stealing her morning newspaper.) Her third marriage was to a Jordanian national who needed a wife in order to stay in the U.S.

"I married for a third time to a young Jordanian student," she said. "He had cousins in countries that he was afraid he'd be forced to fight against. This touched my heart and I figured 'What's the big deal?'"

They divorced after a few years when the student decided to marry his own childhood sweetheart.

She married a fourth time to a "con man" named Dereck who introduced her to his gay lover.

At some point, Andrea did give birth to a third child but put the baby up for adoption in 1961.

ACTING CAREER

In her mid-20s, Andrea got a few acting gigs, landing parts in M*A*S*H, Bewitched and the Russ Meyer T&A classic Beyond the Valley of the Dolls. She would be credited under the name of Samantha

Scott but would also use pseudonyms of Donna Duzzit, Sarah Stunning, and Prudence Smythe.

"She had been a bit player in a lot of TV shows and movies," Riverside County prosecutor James Hawkins said. "She had some beautiful photographs of herself. Facial, bathing suit, different costumes. She was in plays, movies."

Andrea got roles in some late 1960s "nudie cuties" like Horny Hobo, Wild Gypsies, Nude Django and Bad Girls for the Boys. She did manage two get a two episode run as "Betty" in the show Bewitched which would be the high water mark for her in Hollywood.

"She really couldn't make it as an actress," crime author Diane Fanning said. "So she ended up working as a call girl to make money."

Andrea had been thrown off a horse while filming a b-movie. She injured her back and claimed that this forced her into prostitution.

HIGH-PRICED CALL GIRL & DRUGS

"I was finally dating!" she said recalling her decision to become a call-girl. "I had read all Harold Robbins' books to learn about men and a lot of my dreams did come true through with these 'pay dates.'"

According to her probation report, Andrea began using marijuana in her late twenties and used until 1980. She also indulged in barbiturates and morphine based pain medication after she injured her back in the fall of the horse. During her time as a call-girl, she would use cocaine.

MORE MEN

In March of 1980, she married another man after a whirlwind ten-day courtship. The marriage did not last two weeks as her husband went into a jealous rage. Andrea was able to fend him off with a butcher knife, chasing him out of their Los Angeles apartment.

"Andrea was an exceptionally beautiful woman," forensic psychologist Oscar Newsome said. "I mean absolutely beautiful. She knew how to use her body and looks and words to seduce men and get them to do things for her. She was in several relationships and marriages, all short and quick."

DESPERATION TIME

Now in her late 30s, Andrea knew her days as a high-priced call girl would be numbered. She had to meet a "sugar daddy" and fast.

Enter lumber magnate Robert Sand, who at 69 years old was 30 years Andrea's senior.

"Robert Sand had been a lumberman in the northeast," Hawkins said. "He made a fortune there. Retired to Los Angeles. He also had a long standing history with prostitutes."

Sand had been confined to a wheelchair for years. He suffered from multiple sclerosis and was confined to a wheelchair.

Sand had married his first wife Frances in 1939 but they would divorce in 1947. Five years later, they would remarry. She first found out about her husband's proclivities for prostitutes in 1973 which effectively ended their sexual relationship but not the marriage.

"His wife was divorcing him because he had an $800 a week prostitute habit," Fanning said. "And she was just not comfortable with that and she leaves him. So that's how Andrea comes in Bob Sands life."

By December of 1980, Sand had finalized his divorce with Frances. Then he began living with Andrea.

The rich businessman found the sexy former actress and model irresistible. He booked her for repeated engagements as Andrea gave him sex and massages.

"It got to the point where it got so expensive that his accountant recommended that he stopped spending money on her each month and marry her," Hawkins said. "To save money."

"There was the sizable age difference, of course," forensic psychologist Oscar Newsome said. "And the two were introduced by Andrea's 'madam'. So obviously we're not talking the ideal marriage here. It is an arrangement at best."

The madam informed Andrea that Sand sometimes "played rough" but treated the women he sent to her well "in general."

Andrea's fourth divorce became final in December of 1980 and she then moved into Sand's apartment in Westwood where he asked for her hand in marriage. Andrea said "yes" and they moved to a condo at The Springs in Rancho Mirage.

"They lived in a big, gorgeous home," Fanning said. "In a very wealthy area in Rancho Mirage."

"Rancho Mirage is where a lot of political figures, CEOs, and actress and actors retire," Hawkins said. "Its known as the playground of the presidents."

RESPECTABILITY

Sand provided Andrea what she always wanted, respectability and security. They had famous people in their neighborhood like Tammy Faye Baker. So in the beginning, Andrea enjoyed herself.

She wheeled Robert around in his wheelchair as he watched her play golf and tennis. He took her shopping and she would continue to give him therapeutic massages.

"She did have a power over men," Hawkins said. "She had a way about her. She was very sensual. And she would, for lack of a better term, suck you in."

"Andrea Claire was pushing 40 years old," Newsome said. "She had to have seen the writing on the wall when it came to her stripping and call girl days. She wanted the easy life. The rich life. So when she came across Robert Sand she put her best foot forward. Here was a guy, stuck in a wheelchair and had literally money to burn. Most importantly, she knew that he had multiple sclerosis which would only get worse as time went on. She saw him as an opportunity. Marry the old man, wait until he becomes invalid or dies off then enjoy the benefits of his wealth."

CONTROL FREAK

Robert limited Andrea's social life, however. He was a sexual voyeur and made Andrea pose nude for photograph sessions and walk around their condo naked.

"Robert was an old man confined in a wheelchair," Newsome said. "So like most men in that position, he did not want any kind of competition for Andrea. So he kept her confined to the house. They wouldn't go out to eat. He wouldn't let her out, period. She rebelled, of course, but he really want her to be his on-call sex toy."

According to Andrea, Robert liked to spank her with a paddle and masturbated while he watched her have sex with other men. Andrea claimed that Robert became more and more demanding with his requests and fantasies. Every day the envelope was pushed further and further.

"I think her life would drastically change due to a marital contract that we found," Hawkins said. "She agreed to perform sexual services for him. There was a whole list of them. Some of them somewhat perverted. And he would follow her around and photograph her doing everything."

Robert's demands would be increasingly kinky as the months wore on.

"According to Andrea," Fanning said. "Bob got more and more sexually demanding. And the sex that he wanted was more and more sadistic."

MUTUAL ABUSE?

Robert would have complaints of his own, however. He informed his attorney friend that Andrea would routinely berate and insult him as well as leave him alone for long periods as she went off to "play tennis" and that she had a "terrible temper."

"Sand would complain that Andrea would be abusive," Newsome said. "It is unclear whether or not she would initiate the fights with him or she was responding to his own increasing demands. What is clear is that he got more than he bargained for when he married her as he didn't expect her to fight back or display such a temper."

Robert Sand, however, was not going to throw away a Rolls Royce just because it had a few dents in it.

"But he was also compelled to stay with her because she had the most incredible body he'd ever seen," Hawkins said. "And the sex was wonderful."

POISON THE OLD MAN?

With the arrangement becoming more and more intolerable, Andrea contacted a friend and asked him about the effects of Seconal. She said she had already tried to poison Robert and that it didn't work. She also told her tennis partner that her husband would soon die from multiple sclerosis. Her friend said that multiple sclerosis would not kill her husband, Andrea said, "No. He knows he's going to die very soon."

"Andrea had been a sexual plaything all of her life since the age of 15," Newsome said. "She saw Sand as her only way out and yet this was not going to be as easy as she thought. She began to feel resentful at first then it turned into outright hatred. The sexual games that he made her play, paddle boarding, sadomasochism. For even the most hardened prostitute, it all became too much for her."

"That may have been the straw that broke the camel's back," Hawkins said.

Andrea had enough. She wanted a marriage of convenience from a rapidly dying old man. Instead, she got nightly sexual humiliations from wheelchair bound pervert who didn't want a wife. He wanted a sex slave.

"She thought it would be a life of luxury," Hawkins said. "Instead it was a life of somewhat sexual slavery and she just couldn't stand it anymore. Even though Mr. Sand was in a wheelchair I think he was a very demanding person and he exorcised control over her primarily financially."

THE ATTACK

One night in May of 1981 it all came to a head.

Bob Sand laid on the bed, screaming at Andrea to come into the room and perform her sexual duties.

Andrea, however, had something else in mind.

"That's when she attacked him with the knife," Fanning said.

"It was an out of control frenzy," Hawkins said. "Just stabbing over and over and over again. He was stabbed over 27 times and importantly he was stabbed in the heart and severed the aorta."

"The attack was 'overkill' as one psychiatrist at the time described it," Newsome said. "She stabbed the man over twenty-seven times so this was a hate-filled, raging attack of someone who had a high amount of pent-up anger. All the rage and frustration Andrea felt at the humiliation she suffered, hell, maybe all of the rage she suffered for her whole life bubbled to the surface the moment she started stabbing Robert. And she didn't stop there. She picked up a wooden board that she used for exercise and slammed it down on his head so hard that it caused a fracture."

On May 14th, 1981 at 4 o'clock in the morning, security guards at The Springs investigated an alarm coming from the Sands' address. They found the front door open and were soon greeted by an upset Andrea in a black robe. She told the guards that there was a male intruder in the home and he had run out of the sliding glass door in the living room.

She led the guards into the bedroom where they saw the bloodied, nude body of Robert Sand.

Forty-five minutes later, Sheriff's Detective Fred Lastar arrived and the scene was secured. Andrea repeated the story of the intruder and she was allowed to go visit a neighbor.

Investigators would later establish that Sand had been stabbed 27 times and had been hit over the head several times with a 1' x 4' exercise board. There was in fact a trail of blood from the bedroom to the living room's sliding glass door but they found only a single bloodstain on the patio.

There were no footprints on the grass where Andrea said the intruder escaped.

Lastar also found it odd that in the master bathroom above the toilet there was a wet-t-shirt poster of Andrea with her nipples visible under the thin material.

Andrea would tell the Sheriff that she had taken some sleeping pills and had gone to bed early the previous night. She had heard her husband screaming for help and when she investigated she saw one or two men running out of the house.

"She said she heard her husband yelling out," Hawkins said. "She went down the hallway to his bedroom, she saw some stranger in the dark who bumped into her, pushed her out of the way and ran out of the condominium. She went in there to find Robert on the ground."

She looked and saw that Robert was dead. Oddly, she went and washed her clothes when they had gotten bloodied after she tried to help her husband. Even more strangely, Andrea then went back to sleep for two hours before calling security.

"The problem with Andrea's plan was that not only was she a bad actress," Newsome said. "She was a lousy screenwriter. She came up with this half-cocked story of intruders breaking in and stabbing her husband. Sand is a well-to-do retiree. The intruder takes nothing and leaves the buxom actress all alone to sort things through. Right away, the Sheriffs doubted her story. She implored for them to go out looking for the intruder but they found no signs of forced entry. Nothing that would indicate that a stranger had entered their home for the sole purpose of killing a rich old man in a wheelchair."

No weapon was found in the condo but after a re-examination of the place the police found a four-inch kitchen knife under the couch. The autopsy would reveal that the knife was the murder weapon. When this was revealed to Andrea she went and "prayed" and then would declare that she took the knife out of Sand's chest. She claimed she washed both the knife and her clothes.

Laster then asked Andrea if she were willing to take a lie detector test and she refused. At this point, he considered her to be the prime suspect.

The attack on Sand was brutal. The autopsy revealed that the fatal wounds had been to his aorta. He displayed defensive wounds on his arms and wounds which meant that he had been conscious and trying to ward off the attack. The autopsy physician surmised that Sand had been lying down when the attack took place.

PSYCHOTHERAPY

Andrea consulted with her therapist, Dr. Morton Kurland, and he told her to stop talking to the police and get an attorney. He recommended Gary Scherotter, considered the best criminal attorney in Palm Springs.

Andrea heeded his advice despite the fact it was quickly looking like she was a black widow on the prowl for a rich husband to kill.

A TURN FOR THE BIZARRE

On July 23rd, the Indio Sheriff's department received an emergency call from Andrea Sand's residence.

When police arrived they found Andrea nude on the kitchen floor. Her hands and feet were tied behind her and a knife was stuck in her buttocks.

She told the police that she had returned home after a visit to New Jersey. She stated that two men and a woman had tied her up and repeatedly raped her.

During the rape, the intruders informed her that they had murdered her husband and would be back for more.

"The police came into her home," Fanning said. "She was bound hand and foot. And she had a knife sticking out of her buttocks."

"We never found any evidence of the assault," Hawkins said. "We couldn't find any physical evidence on her."

Detective Chris Brown realized that the rope had been tied with slipknots and there was the possibility that Andrea had tied herself up. During an interview with Andrea, Brown stated that he doubted Andrea's story.

"If you don't believe me, why don't you arrest me?" Andrea challenged.

"It's possible you'll be arrested," Brown said. "Based on my past experience, one of three things is going to happen. You'll either kill yourself, kill someone else, or I'll have another call back here for another phony situation."

MORE "ATTACKS"

Andrea began calling the sheriffs on a regular basis, stating that the same intruders came and raped her again.

"She continued to tell us that the intruders returned, kidnapped and sexually assaulted her repeatedly. There were so many incidents."

She also produced numerous threatening letters which she claimed were from the gang of murderers/rapists.

The letters were determined to be fakes as the only fingerprints on the paper belonged to Andrea herself.

"I've been on the bench for fifteen years," Hawkins said. "And I haven't seen any cases as bizarre as this one.

"In all of her alleged attacks," Newsome said. "Andrea was always the victim. There was never any physical evidence or signs of forced entry. These were phantom intruders. She was tested for DNA and they found nothing. So the police knew that they were dealing with someone who was either schizophrenic or making the lamest attempt to throw them off her trail. Amazing that she had so little foresight into what she was doing. Like a bad screenwriter, she had no one to bounce her bizarre ideas off of so she ended up doing a lot of bizarre things that only tightened the noose around her own neck."

FINDING A NEW MAN

True to the pattern of her life, Andrea could not go long without a new man by her side. She would meet Joe Mack Mims at a Christmas party at the Evangelical Free Church. Mims was 56 years old, widowed and a water pump consultant.

Andrea had a neighbor who encouraged her to "find Jesus" and she came into the church of Mims who was a regular attendee of the services there.

Mims became enamored with Andrea and believed her stories about the murder of her ex-husband and the repeated attacks. He went so far as to visit the Deputy D.A. Jim Hawkins and complained that if they knew anything about police work they "would probably have the murderer by now."

Mims then informed Hawkins that he was going to marry Andrea. Hawkins advised Mims against this, stating that they were going to charge her with the murder of Sand.

"Go ahead and charge her," Mims replied. "I'm still going to marry her."

"He became irate," Hawkins said. "He suggested that I spend my time trying to find the intruders that keep returning and assaulting her. And stop harassing her."

"Mims had a classic case of 'Captain Save-A-Ho,'" Newsome said. "Here was this woman who has worked as a call-girl, has two children, has been married five times and he is naïve enough to believe that after listening to a few sermons she is a changed woman. So he becomes her savior, marches down to the police station to intimidate them, marches down to the D. A's office. All the while, Andrea is not saying a word. She has a new man to do her bidding, to plead her case. She's damn good at finding these kind of men. She had been doing it her whole life."

FIRST DEGREE MURDER CHARGES

On March 25th, 1982, Andrea's attorney Gary Scherotter was notified by the D.A.'s office that Andrea would be charged with first degree murder. Scherotter sent her to the court where she posted $100,000 bail and was set free.

The next day, Andrea and Joe Mims were married.

SIXTH TIME IS A CHARM?

Andrea did not want to sell the condo at The Springs until Sand's estate was settled. Mims sold his own home and moved in with Andrea at The Springs.

"He took it upon himself to try and protect her from the return of the intruders who kept kidnapping and assaulting her," Hawkins said.

"Again, the poor guy is smitten by her charms," Newsome said. "Here is a 56-year old man living as an anonymous life as possible. He meets a woman sixteen years his junior. She's stunning, she's posed in Playboy, been in movies and now she is reformed at the church of his choice. He's convinced she's in love with him and is willing to move heaven and earth to make protect that illusion."

MORE BIZARRE STUNTS

Two months later after they were married, however, Mims called the police and informed them that Andrea had been kidnapped. The officers began a search but Andrea returned home on the same day claiming she had been abducted and raped by the same intruders as before.

No physical evidence was found but Mims remained steadfast in his belief that Andrea was telling the truth.

Andrea was able to put on a false front with Mims, appearing to genuinely care about the man as they would engage in social gatherings at church.

But on Halloween of 1982, Andrea convinced Mims that they should take a drive together. They drove along Highway 74 and turned into an isolated dirt road. Andrea threw a bed sheet on the gravel and began to give Mims fellatio.

Mims climaxed into her mouth after which she spit his semen into a tissue. She then told him to roll over on his stomach and she would give him a massage.

"So Joe thinks this is the best thing going," Fanning said

Mims was like putty under her expert hands but then something hit him hard on the back of the head.

He screamed in pain until he was hit again.

Turning around, he saw Andrea holding a hammer, wanting to hit him again. He pushed her off and grabbed her arm, ripping the hammer out of her grip.

"What in the name of God are you doing?" he asked.

"I've got to knock you out so that people will believe I've been raped."

Mims finally saw the light. He knew that she had thought to use the semen in the tissue to provide evidence she had been raped.

"The fact that she tried to kill him (Mims) was a real game changer," Hawkins said. "The evidence that we needed to really go forward on the case."

KNOCKED INTO COMING INTO HIS SENSES

Mims dressed and drove Andrea home before going to the hospital to get his head stitched up.

The next morning, Mims moved out of the condo. He notified authorities of the assault, prompting an attempted murder charge to be added to the first degree case against Andrea.

Mims moved to have his marriage with Andrea annulled. Andrea's bail was then revoked and she went to jail to await the trial.

Andrea's attorney, Gary Scherotter, now believed that she wasn't mentally stable and had the court examine her for competency. Andrea was taken to Riverside General Hospital for observation and tried to commit suicide twice during her stay there by slashing her wrists.

"Her whole world finally came crashing down," Newsome said. "She was completely out of control. A psychologically broken woman with no way out and no answers, she finally broke down and tried to end it all."

MENTALLY COMPETENT

Scherotter would resign as her attorney as the Sand estate had been tied up in litigation and she could no longer afford to pay him. Andrea was appointed a public defender in Charles Stafford who changed Andrea's please from not guilty to not guilty by reason of insanity. His defense lay in the hopes that the jury would believe that Andrea had been driven crazy by the men in her life who abused her and it all came to a blowout when Robert Sand forced her to be the victim in his bizarre, sadomasochistic fantasies.

But the prosecution found a man named Richard Cordine who was a convict serving a twelve year sentence for robbery at a Nevada State Prison. Cordine stated that Andrea had started a pen pal relationship with him in 1977 which continued for years until Joe Mims found out about it and stopped it. Cordine would testify that Andrea called him after the Sand murder and confessed "I stabbed the bastard."

Her prosecutor, Robert Dunn, would call her a "malingerer who would lie to achieve her own end." He dismissed the idea of Andrea killing Sand out of self-defense on the grounds that Robert was a paraplegic.

"She planned Sand's murder to get money from his will," Dunn said. "She received about $150,000 in cash and $100,000 equity in the couple's condominium."

"She stabbed the man twenty-seven times," Newsome said. "This scared the crap out of the jurors. Andrea would take the stand and give the performance of her life by recounting her tales of abuse but in the end, it was those twenty-seven stab wounds that stayed in the mind of the jurors."

After deliberation, a ten-woman, two man jury found Andrea Mims guilty of first degree murder. The judge sentenced her to 26 years to life and sent her to the California Institute for Women in Frontera.

"When the judge read the verdict to her," Fanning said. "She slammed down a box of tissues on the thing (table) and said 'I killed him because he called me a whore!'"

"Manipulation always worked for Andrea," Newsome said. "She knew how to manipulate men all her life. She thought she could manipulate everyone else the same way, cops, jurors, telling them about her tales of abuse and woe and thereby mitigating her own culpability in all the bad things she did.

REMARRIAGE?

Joe Mims tried to jump start his life after Andrea was sentenced but could not seem to get over her. He knew that she had killed Robert Sand but also believed she had been forced to do it as her attorney had claimed. He then heard a radio program discussing PMS and concluded that Andrea had suffered from the condition when she killed her husband and attacked him.

Mims did research on PMS then visited Andrea in prison, telling her of his findings. Andrea requested progesterone from the jailhouse doctor but the physician found no symptoms of PMS. He finally gave in to her demands, however, and the drug seemed to improve her demeanor.

Andrea displayed good behavior in prison. Mims had a renewed hope that he would get a new trial for Andrea on the basis of his PMS theory. He proposed marriage once again and Andrea accepted. He wrote love letters to Andrea such as the one below:

"My Darling Drea,

I promise you a love that will be true, I will always put you first in my life. I will do all I can to meet your every need, while we are apart it will be hard, but our God will bring you home to me. I love you with all my heart,

Your Hubby,

Joe"

On May 13th, 1986, Mims showed up at the prison to marry Andrea. He never made it past the front gate, however, as he began to experience chest pain then collapse. He was transported to to Chino Community Hospital where he was pronounced dead of a heart attack.

After Mims' death, Andrea once again reiterated her story that intruders had killed Robert Sand.

During her prison term she became a prolific artist at the Central California Women's facility and won several awards as well as becoming a Buddhist.

"I'm very proud of my achievements," she said in a prison newsletter. "I've used the past 20 plus years to improve myself, learning to grow in a positive way and also to heal and forgive myself."

Andrea was paroled in 2012 but suffered from ovarian cancer which soon got into her lungs. She would die at the Mesa Verde Convalescent Hospital in Costa Mesa, CA.

"I do understand that she suffered at the hands of men," Hawkins said. "Why she had the relationship problems that she did but I don't think that was ever an excuse to forgive or forget what she did to Robert Sand."

AMNESIAC KILLER : THE TRUE STORY OF DANIELLE STEWART

119

LES ACKERMAN

"I would punish all of those who had never lost anything, those who had never had anything taken away from them. I would let the anger from my chest reach out and explode in spectacular violence." - An excerpt from a poem by Danielle Stewart

Danielle Stewart had a normal and happy childhood until around the age of seven. Both of her parents were public servants and the family lived in the Curtin, Canberra region of Australia. She had one younger sister and the family seemed en route to living a normal, happy life.

Danielle was particularly close to her father during her childhood years. He took her swimming, read books to her at night and sang to her. She described him as being a man with a great sense of humor and the kind of man who "did all the things that dads do."

At the age of seven, however, Danielle's life took a traumatic turn. Her family was building a holiday house in the NSW south coast town of Batemans Bay. Danielle, unfortunately, came into the cross hairs of a sexual predator.

The man was a neighbor and Danielle would come over to his home to watch TV as they had no television of their own in their holiday house. The man was a married real estate agent in his 50s. He would let Danielle and a friend come with him to outings where they would examine unoccupied houses he was selling. It was there, inside these homes, that the assaults would take place.

Danielle would be under the man's spell for over three years before they molestations came to an end.

When she was eleven years old, tragedy struck again in the form of losing her mother to cancer. Distraught, her father sent her away for a weekend with a friend of a family. The family had a teenaged son, however, who constantly harassed Danielle, molesting her as well.

Her father would remarry six months later to a woman who had three children of her own. Danielle felt betrayed by her father's remarriage and tried to commit suicide with an overdose of pills. Her father himself had suffered from depression and fell apart emotionally after the death of Danielle's mother.

"I've always believed that depression and mental illness is inheritable," forensic psychologist Pauline Malloy said. "Sometimes through genetics, sometimes through thought processes. With Danielle, she clearly inherited some mental illness from her father's side of the family as her dad suffered from depression as well as her paternal grandfather."

Her maternal grandparents arrived and offered that Danielle come live with them. Danielle didn't want to go, she wanted to stay with her Dad but her father didn't want her screwing up the dynamics of his new family with her bad behavior.

He wanted her gone.

So Danielle was given two choices, either go live with her grandparents or go to a youth shelter.

Danielle chose to run away

"Danielle suffered numerous traumas, back to back," Malloy said. "The loss of her innocence, the loss of her mom and then the rejection of her father. Any of the above could have been cause for life altering psychological trauma but she suffered all of these within a four year time span. It had to crush her psychically and she did not have the life experience to cope."

Running away, the twelve year old girl roughed it out on the streets. Finally, she grew tired and returned home to her father. She would not be treated as the prodigal daughter, however, as her father had her bags packed and waiting. He drove Danielle to a local youth shelter and dropped her off.

Danielle would remain there for the next three months.

Danielle did not like the youth refuge. There was a lot of drug use, alcohol and she once again experienced sexual abuse.

"This was a horrid life for her at this point," Malloy said. "At some point I think she broke down psychologically and the seeds for future violent behavior were planted here."

RETURNING HOME

She eventually returned home to live with her father but he had settled in with his new family.

"I felt so alone, unloved, misunderstood," Danielle recalled. "and as the problems at home got worse, I got worse. I was sneaking out of the house, drinking, drugging. I missed my mum so terribly, I just wanted to be with her."

Danielle would attempt suicide on several occasions, leaving permanent scars on her wrist.

"I used a razor in my bedroom downstairs," Danielle said. "There was no internet back then and I didn't know how to do it [properly]."

On her 13th birthday, her father celebrated by throwing her out of the house once again. She would go and live with her friend Elle O'Brien and her mother. O'Brien's mother fed her and took her in, allowing the unwanted girl to remain there for four years.

At the age of sixteen, she enrolled at Narrabundah College and become a student of renowned poet Geoff Page.

"She was leagues ahead of anyone I've encountered writing contemporary poetry at that age," Page recalled. "She had some of the same virtues as Sylvia Plath, a real feeling for adventurous imagery. There was a lot going on in her brain at an intense level and she had the talent to turn it into something moving."

Under the guidance of her teacher, Danielle published an anthology of poems called "I for Icarus."

Danielle would go on to study performing arts at Melbourne's Monash University before traveling to Sydney to share an apartment with her step-sister, Myfanwy Thompson. Both young women would indulge in alcohol and prescription drugs, becoming the catalyst for each others self-destructive behavior. Myfanwy, however, would suffer a freak accident in falling off a cliff while taking ecstasy.

The loss devastated Danielle as she considered Myfanwy to be her best friend.

"Her boyfriend had got into dealing ecstasy," Danielle said. "I couldn't handle seeing her wasted all the time, so I'd moved out with other friends."

Her younger step-brother, Tristram would later die of an aneurysm after being diagnosed with schizophrenia.

MEANDERING THROUGH LIFE

Danielle was now 24 and wandered aimlessly through life. She went from one job to the next until she met the 50-year old Chaim Kimel in late 2000.

"They met on the dance floor and hit it off immediately," journalist Byron Kaye said.

Despite the age difference, Chaim Kamel was a stylish man with his own business.

"He was a bit of a bon vivant," crime author Paul Kidd said. "Lived in the good part of Sydney. A good lifestyle."

"He was very charismatic, very gregarious, very charming, very generous, strong and creative," Danielle said. "He loved his children and they loved him."

Kimel had been a successful entrepreneur, dealing in antiques. She got a job working for Chaim in his furniture store, Eclectica in Mosman. Kimel had put Danielle in charge of bookkeeping.

The two got along exceptionally well, at first, with common interests in art, music, and food.

"Danielle was a very attractive," Kidd said. "Petite, blonde, loved to drink. He (Chaim) was an older man but a really good style of a bloke."

The relationship started platonic in the beginning.

"He made some advances which weren't initially reciprocated," Kaye said. "But over time, they became intimate and it was on."

Kimel thought Danielle was a "prize catch". He invited Danielle over to visit his family and she was impressed with how close and living they were. There she saw, for the first time since her early childhood, a loving family that she could be a part of.

Danielle moved in with Kimel who had the time lived with his ten year old son Jordan. He also had a daughter, Amber and Fred, who were in their early twenties and late teens respectively.

A CHANGE IN DEMEANOR?

One of her friends, however, thought that Danielle changed after she met Chaim. She described him as being very possessive and told her what to do.

"I loved him," Danielle said. "I still do. It is a love-hate thing and it won't ever go. With those types of personalities, there is that level of attention, you become their entire focus."

Danielle would have these kind of intense relationships all of her life and it seemed to be the fuel to her fire. She was irresistibly drawn to the drama and would have it on full blast with Chaim Kimel.

"Anyone who would have been in a relationship with Danielle Stewart would have been in a relationship that was doomed from the start," Kidd said. "The combination of psychological problems fueled by excesses of alcohol was always going to end in disaster."

COCAINE AND BOOZE

Danielle began substance abuse at an early age which only progressed as she got older. She now had a benefactor in Chaim as well as an enabler as he liked to party, indulging in cocaine himself.. He didn't realize, however, that the alcohol would only stoke the flames that would extinguish their relationship.

He also had a dark side, according to Danielle's grandmother. She described him as someone who was "demanding and overpowering."

"She (Danielle) went through life with a paranoia that people were going to leave her," Kidd said. "And she became very, very possessive of her partner and that fueled by alcohol was the basis of the majority of their problems."

CALL THE POLICE

Once the relationship turned intimate, things started getting out of hand. The two indulged in alcohol and had numerous fights in which the police were called in.

Danielle had been taking strong anti-depression medications and mixing these drugs with alcohol. One fight had gotten so severe that she took a restraining order out against Kimel.

On one occasion, Kimel violated the order and was jailed for one night.

"I'd moved into temporary accommodation and Chaim came after me," Danielle said. "He broke into my room and stole my laptop and wallet. The police busted him on the way out and took him to jail for the night."

Kimel explained to the police that he violated the order because Danielle had called him stating that she had swallowed fourteen Valiums.

"I'm fine when I'm not in an emotional situation," Danielle said, "but when I'm under threat, the flashbacks can be extreme."

"She (Danielle) had a borderline personality disorder," Malloy said. "When things go bad with her, they go real bad. That was how she lived her entire life up until that point. She had to engage in fights, drinking, drugs. Drama, drama, drama. If it isn't there, she will create it."

A PROPENSITY FOR VIOLENCE

Kimel's son, Jordan, was ten years old when his father first met Danielle. He recalled Danielle as a destructive psychotic stating that she would "cut up $10,000 worth of business suits, delete important documents from my father's computer. Once, she punched through a glass bathroom window and slashed her wrists. And she'd punch my father, too."

"Unfortunately, this was the pattern that was set," Malloy set. "They would argue, fight and then get back together. When they would get back together things would be more passionate and clingy than before. 'Please, don't leave me,' that sort of thing. But then the cycle repeats itself and it has to be more extreme in order for the couple to get that same 'high.'"

The couple would remain together and make attempts to appear respectable. In 2004, Danielle enrolled at a nearby college to finish her degree while they both started an online catering company called Epicurean. The money to start the company was borrowed from Danielle's grandmother, a total of $30,000.

Later that year, the couple would journey to India where they would marry at the Taj Mahal.

Danielle would claim, however, that the money the borrowed for the business is what kept her in the marriage .

"Part of the reason I married Chaim was because I was worried about my grandparents' money," Danielle said. "If I left him, there'd be no legal recourse for me to get it back. He took it without shame; he never planned to pay it back."

"Typical of people with borderline personality disorders," Malloy said. "Is that they have to play the role of the victim. It is a head scratcher as to why Chaim would borrow thirty-grand when he had his own business. Maybe he thought he would be placating her somehow with them being in business together and having her feel as if she were a part of things. But clearly he didn't need anything more on his plate."

BOOMERANG BABY

Danielle would leave Kimel a total of seven times during their seven year relationship. She would confide in her grandmother and friend Elle, saying she was unhappy. Then he would call and they would get back together.

"It (their relationship) was very alcohol fueled," Kaye said. "Very hedonistic. A lot of violent arguments."

Danielle blamed her inability to stay away from Chaim on her lack of self-esteem.

"While he could be caring, it was undermined by his desire to keep me enslaved to him," Danielle said. "When I left him, he'd follow me and get me back. When your sense of self-esteem is so low and a learnt helplessness has set in, you don't feel able to support yourself. My friends had dropped off because they couldn't stand him. The only times I responded with violence were when I was trying to leave and he'd try to stop me. He'd hide my wallet, phone, computer, passport. Those times always ended with me being in hospital, not him. I never tried to kill him: I tried to kill myself."

WHO WAS ABUSING WHO?

It became apparent to Kimel's family, however, that he had married a woman prone to violent outbursts. Kimel told his daughter than Danielle had bitten him on his thumb and arm as as smashing his glasses.

He had his glasses broken so much that it had become a "running joke", according to his daughter Amber.

After arguments, Danielle would delete Kimel's emails and computer files. Kimel had became so enraged at her actions that he kicked her out of the house. Danielle would return, kicking out the timber door.

WELCOME TO THE PSYCH WARD

Danielle had overdosed on medication numerous times during the course of her marriage. She would inform doctors that Kimel was controlling and that she had "nothing to live for."

His daughter, Amber, however, expressed concern for her father's well being and wanted him to sever ties with Danielle.

"He told me he'd made a commitment to be there for her and loved her unconditionally," Amber said. "He was convinced unconditional love would cure her."

"Chaim was the rescuer," Malloy said. "He couldn't help himself. Danielle was the beautiful damsel in distress. They had passionate sex together, he knew about her past, and he couldn't be another man that brought more pain in her life. He didn't want that. He thought that through his own sincerity and love that he could somehow bring her to a place of healing. But he wasn't a professional. And that isn't what relationships are for."

A NEW MAN

In 2006, Danielle separated from Kimel and met Melbourne university professor Joeri Mol. She moved in with him and became pregnant by December of that year. Danielle wanted to go back to Sydney, however, and didn't want to raise the child with Mol as a single mother.

"She went out with somebody else," Kaye said. "He was seeing other people but they could not stop speaking. They remained extremely close. The new fellow (Mol) wants to settle down and start raising a family. Which incidentally was Danielle's greatest dream, which was to have a family. But she's still drawn to Chaim uncontrollably."

A week later, she called Kimel and the two met to discuss a reconciliation.

"He (Chaim) told her that either she as a termination," Kidd said. "Or there's no hope if them ever getting back together."

She complied with his request, her second abortion in six months (the first with Kimel) and she once again went into a depression.

"Danielle desperately wanted to experience the happiness that she had before her mother died," Malloy said. "She always told her grandmother, 'I just want have a normal life. I just want to have a normal life.' What she really wanted was that family again. So now she spends her life grasping at straws, going from this man to that man, and getting multiple abortions."

BURNING THE CANDLE AT BOTH ENDS

The couple moved back in together in 2007 but this time their break-up would be much more volatile.

And violent.

"It was short lived (their reconciliation)," Kidd said. "Now that they were back together. It was business as usual."

Business as usual was a lot of fighting and alcohol coupled with a flurry of activity to keep up with the bills.

Danielle returned to college and continued to run their catering business, The Epicurean. In order to make ends meet, however, she took a part time job at a Sydney ad agency.

She couldn't juggle all of these things at once, so she turned to cocaine and alcohol. Her friends described her as "withdrawn" and "unsettled" after meeting with her after the latest reconciliation.

Danielle began to feel the itch to run away again, telling friends she now just wanted to earn some money on her own and get away from Kimel for good.

"How the hell could this have worked to begin with?" Malloy said. "You've got a woman with some serious issues, abused by men, abandoned as a child and now she's an alcoholic with major depression. The pattern is set in their relationship. Break-up, get back together, fight some more. Rinse and repeat. This can only end badly. The question was, how bad?"

THE FATEFUL DINNER

"The old problems kept resurfacing," Kaye said. "They kept on with the dinner parties. Living the good life. And with this came Danielle's terrible response to alcohol access."

On August 23rd of 2007, Danielle went out with Kimel to have dinner at a restaurant called Pescador. They were described in a police statement by their friend, Angela Batley, to be in "good spirits."

"It is noted by others there that Danielle seemed a little drunker than usual," Kaye said. "Things got a little bit more testy and Danielle left and decided to walk home."

After dinner, Chaim went with his friends to Angela Batley's home. He would call Danielle from the home and she said that she would come and pick him up. Things took a turn for the strange when Danielle came over but drove back without Chaim who ended up walking home.

Batley was concerned about the tenseness of the situation and called Kimel to make sure he got home safe. Kimel told Batley that Danielle was working on the computer but was "drunk" and that he had to go.

Danielle arrived at their home before Kimel. She told the 16-year old Jordan that she "shouldn't have gone to Angela's house. I've had too much to drink."

Jordan stated that Danielle began playing loud music through the computer, dancing with a drink in her hand. When Kimel arrived, he told her to turn the music down before the neighbors start complaining. An argument ensued before Kimel turned off Danielle's music himself. The argument escalated, the topics being the loud music then escalating to the fact that Chaim would change the password on the computer, which was an ongoing issue in their relationship.

She started to physically attack him but Chaim easily evaded the rushes of the drunk Danielle. Then in the heat of the moment, she picked up one of Chaim's antique ornamental knives he had on display. Chaim came forward, ordering her to place the knife down, then she stuck it into his stomach.

Chaim fell to the ground and she stabbed him again.

"They were both yelling for about 15 minutes," stated Jordan. "All of a sudden, I could hear them in the corridor outside my room. It sounded like someone was being hit or punched and I heard my father say, 'Why are you being violent and attacking me?' They kept fighting and I heard Danielle fall to the floor and scream. Soon after this, I heard my father say in a tense voice, 'What are you doing? Are you crazy?' I heard my father scream three times. I saw [his] white shirt was covered in blood all up the left side from underneath his ribs towards the middle of his torso. Danielle was standing about two metres away and she had our antique knife in her hand."

Jordan saw his father struggling to get to the front door. He was covered in blood and Danielle was hysterical, holding up the knife.

"So the son runs out of his room," Kaye said. "He finds his father clutching his stomach where he's been stabbed twice. Covered in blood. Barely able to speak."

Jordan then thought about attacking Danielle himself.

"He picks up a golf club then thinks for a moment, that he might avenge his father," Kaye said. "It's actually Chaim himself who tells him don't do it. Lying there, sort of holding himself together. The son puts the golf club down and nurses his father while he lies there dying."

Kimel would be rushed to the hospital but die on the operating table at St. Vincent's Hospital, bleeding to death from the two stab wounds to his stomach.

"To the end of his life," Malloy said. "Kimel was protecting Danielle. When his son wanted revenge, he held him back."

Danielle was arrested but plead not guilty on the grounds of self defense. Her blood alcohol reading, however, was five times the legal driving limit.

"It was a stupid, pointless, uncontrolled lover's argument," Kaye said. "And one split second decision led to this terrible outcome."

Danielle maintained no recollection of the events, as she mixed the anti-psychotic drug Seroquel with alcohol. She awoke in a prison cell and called out for her husband, seeing her name on the board with the word 'Murder' written next to it.

"It was the worst moment of my life," Danielle recalled. "In one instant, my entire life had changed and Chaim's had ended."

"Something was going to happen that night," Malloy said. "Her mind was on edge. This may not have been pre-meditated but she knew what was going to happen when she picked up that knife. Remember, she didn't just slash at him as a warning. She thrust the knife into Chaim. Not once. But twice. There was an untapped rage there that came to the surface at the moment. It had been bubbling for a long, long time and unfortunately Chaim Kimel could not foresee how this would end."

THE AFTERMATH

Danielle made a recorded phone call to her father a few days after the killing.

"If I could swap Chaim with me right now, I would do it immediately," Danielle said. "There is no way I meant to kill him."

"Again, I don't think the murder was pre-planned," Malloy said. "But it did seem to be part of Danielle's destiny. What we see here in her killing of Chaim was a metaphor of her own trauma. She was abused by a man in his fifties, molested by him from the ages of seven through ten. She grows into a beautiful woman can choose just about whatever man she wants but instead she elects a man in his fifties, over twenty-five years her senior. That is no coincidence. She is repeating her trauma from the past. But this time she wants to control it. She wants to exorcise the demons of the past so all of those violent fights are trial runs until finally she reaches for that knife and stabs Chaim, metaphorically killing the molester of her past. Now her husband, who actually really loved her, is the victim of this cycle of abuse that has finally come full circle."

Her father agreed to post Danielle's bail but would not agree to the 24-hour surveillance condition attached to it. Her father abandoning her yet again, she turned to her friend Elle O'Brien's mother. She came to bail out Danielle and secured her release after nine months.

Danielle then went to live with her grandmother.

Facing twenty-five years in prison, Danielle would attempt suicide two more times, one of them involving an overdose of Seroquel.

"When I took that Seroquel, I went into psychosis," Danielle said. "It was an out-of-body experience where I thought the nurses were talking about me even though they weren't. I was watching myself from afar. It was crazy, crazy shit. I am sure that is what must have happened on the night Chaim died."

"The psych med plus alcohol defense has become a cliched defense for a lot of killers," Malloy said. "Danielle had done her research. She had studied scriptwriting in school. Everything she said and did had a rehearsed feel to it."

FROM MURDER TO MANSLAUGHTER

The murder charge had been downgraded to manslaughter as Danielle maintained she had no recollection of what happened. She did not remember any of the events of what happened that night not to mention taking the ornamental knife and stabbing her husband with it.

She did not take the stand, however.

"Danielle was charged with murder," Kaye said. "She wept throughout much of the trial. It was very clear that she regretted what she'd done and she wanted him back and she felt quite horrible."

Kimel's children, however, saw Danielle as an imposter the more they investigated the case. They found a synopsis of a play that Danielle had been working on. In the story, one of the characters had a secret desire to kill her older husband.

Fred Kimel, Chaim's oldest son, noted that the play contained details on "jail architecture, prisoner psychology, different cell classifications, prisoner attire, prison visiting hours and life sentences."

The Kimel family once enamored with Danielle, now saw her in a completely different light.

"It was a university assignment, a book I was writing," Danielle said. "I heard that somewhere men kill their partners because they want them to stay, whereas women kill their partners because they want to escape. I know why I was writing about prison: because I was imprisoned long before I was [actually] incarcerated."

SENTENCING

Danielle would be sentenced to six years in prison. She would serve only four.

"There's no doubt that jail saved me," Danielle said. "It prevented me from harming myself with alcohol and drugs. I wouldn't recommend it, though."

During the first nine months of her term, she had been housed in the mental health unit. She could not stop crying. But the prison assigned her to a job in the kitchen and she found her fellow inmates to be helpful.

"I managed to get a few of the heavies on side somehow and avoided the others where possible," Danielle said. "I learnt to assimilate, to hide the fact that I was pretty and educated. I adapted where I could. In jail, I lost everything that made me me: my family, dog, business, house, studies, friends, freedom, clothes, make-up, choices. All I had was myself, my mind and my heart. I learnt to spot evil from a mile away - and evil does exist, I've come face to face with it - but I could still love. This is how I got through jail. Yes, I learnt how to operate within the system, but I could still see beauty in people, and I tried to speak to that."

"Danielle was a well-spoken, educated young woman," Malloy said. "But why the hell would she plead not guilty? She did her research on prison culture beforehand so a cynic can argue that she got off very, very light for what she did. Call it misandry, call it getting the female pass, Danielle was able to get off light for a cold-blooded murderer. She used all of the things from her past to mitigate her own culpability. Sexual abuse, parental death and abandonment down to psych meds and alcohol. She combined those things to get sympathy from Chaim and later from the her jury of her crime."

Danielle walked out of prison on June 24th, 2010.

She is now focused on the prospect of moving to Spain and becoming a professional writer.

"I've paid for what has happened and I've done all I can to fix the issues within myself that contributed to Chaim's death," Danielle said. "I see both a psychiatrist and a psychologist, both of my own volition, nothing to do with parole directives. I don't drink. I don't take drugs. I take responsibility for my actions. I write when I can. I try to love my friends and family. I try to see beauty in the world and I'd like to hope, one day, that I can contribute to that beauty. Still, I love. I still love Chaim. I still love my father. In the end, love will be all I have."

TWISTED SISTERS : THE TRUE STORY OF REGINA AND MARGARET DEFRANCISCO

KORI MAYER

CHAPTER ONE

Regina and Margaret DeFrancisco are two sisters convicted of first degree murder.

On paper, the two sisters look like two girls you would see at a church social.

In school, both were good but not great students. Margaret was the pretty one. She would get all of the attention from the boys but return little interest.

Margaret was a student at Jones College Prep School, a selective public institution that is considered one of the top high schools in Illinois.

A little on the shy side, Margaret had a quick wit and sense of humor. Sweet-looking and pretty, she had avoided any kind of trouble throughout her young life. Her early photos suggest, however, that her subtle smirk was a couldn't contain the narcissism that was growing within.

"You would look at Margaret and see right through her," one of her neighbors said. "It was black, like was nothing there. She didn't seem like she had depth, like she had compassion."

Regina had a love for animals, particularly ponies. She rode horses and in her words, "never lost a show."

Regina was also the more extroverted of the two, wearing her emotions on her sleeve. She could mouth off and had a chip on her shoulder. She also had a thing for 'bad boys', seeing them as a reflection of herself.

"A lot of girls get turned on by the 'thug life'," forensic psychologist Marnie Clark said. "The DeFrancisco sisters definitely fit that mold. They were not out to play Mrs. Cleaver when they grew up. They were attracted to the gang lifestyle. They thought the drama was exciting."

The girls were raised by a single parent, Nora DeFrancisco. Nora raised the two sisters and their brother Joey in the Pilsen neighborhood of Chicago. Their father, Augie DeFrancisco was a small-time burglar and convicted drug dealer who had no involvement in the girl's childhood years. Their maternal grandfather, Gilbert Smith, was a former Chicago cop who was fired from the force in 1960 after admitting that he was "friendly with certain burglars."

Growing up in Pilsen, however, the girls could not avoid rubbing shoulders with gang members. They became enamored with gang culture, learning who fought against who and what the names of the gangs were. There were the Latin Counts, Kool Gang, Villa Lobos, Bishops, among many other offshoots. The girls knew what streets signified what gang members' territory and memorized their hand signals.

"Chicago is simply rife with gangs," Clark said. "It is inescapable, even to those in the more affluent communities. There is still a choice, however. For whatever reason, the DeFrancisco sisters were drawn to the 'thug life'. To a young person, it looks 'cool'.

They are the classic examples of young women who could not see the big picture and thought the thug life was something worth aspiring to."

The two sisters, with their striking brunette looks, could not help but come into the cross hairs of the local gang members. They began wearing dark lipstick and teasing their hair out. Margaret would get a tattoo on her belly. Regina would have the letter "R" tattooed on her leg as well as a drawing of a heart just above her breast. They would hang out on street corners and in front of the local liquor store, chatting up the neighborhood 'gangstas'.

"The changes in their make-up and dress signified the changes in their personality," Clark said. "They grew bored during their time at prep school. Even ashamed. They did not want to see themselves as nerds and hated that aspect of themselves. Starting in eighth grade, it was time to start rebelling. By the time they reached high-school, the thug life was part of their persona. Dark make-up. Tattoos. Hanging out with gang bangers. Alcohol and drugs. But most important, they wanted all the drama that came with that kind of life. Who is out to get who, who dissed who and who shot who became their modus operandi in life."

Grandfather Gilbert, however, had seen this all before as a Chicago cop. He feared that the girls, particularly Regina, would become ensnared by the street gang culture. He tried to obstruct this from happening and found Regina a job with a local periodontist. He figured if he kept the girl busy with school and work it would keep her away from the idiots on the street.

Regina, however, did not have the emotional maturity to see the light. She showed up late for her first couple of shifts then she was fired.

But she had started dating a man named Johnny Rivera, a known member of Chicago's notorious "Latin Kings" street gang. Rivera had a rap sheet as long as "War and Peace" as well as more aliases than a Russian spy

Regina would learn how to package and deal drugs at the foot of Johnny. She would watch him put the cocaine into plastic bags, measuring it out by the ounce. They would drive around town and Johnny would introduce her to his customers, watching as he conducted the deals. The secret handshakes and secret lingo all became apart of Regina's world.

Officially crossing over from innocent prep school girl to drug dealing girlfriend, Regina lived a double life. She did manage to get a part-time job doing data entry work for a local law firm and had enrolled in the local junior college (Harold Washington).

Margaret was getting into trouble as well. Her grades in high school were slipping as she would sneak out at night to be with friends. She would often come to school looking "disheveled" according to one teacher who thought she looked like a child whose parents were going through a divorce.

And there was trouble on the home front.

Neighbors would report hearing the girls fighting with their mother on a daily basis.. The two girls were out of control with no father figure to put them in line. Nora would berate Regina whenever she would act up in school or get arrested and the girls would yell back.

In private, Nora would refer to her daughters as "the bitches".

Things would come to a head when Regina would get arrested for selling cocaine to an undercover cop. A single mom already strapped for cash as she had to support three children on her own, Nora was livid as she paid Regina's bail.

"How are you going to pay me back?" .

"I don't know!"

"Do you know how much it costs to bail you out of jail!" Nora screamed. "You are going to pay me back. You're going to pay me back every penny!"

CHAPTER TWO

"She needs money," Margaret said, her voice full of concern.

"How much?" Oscar asked.

"One thousand dollars. Can you help us out, baby?"

That was the scene set for the twenty-two year old Oscar Velazquez in June of 2000 as he spoke to the sister of his current teenage crush, Regina DeFrancisco. He spotted Regina around the neighborhood of Pilsen and quickly fell for her dark Irish-Italian good looks. Showing off his brand new Z28 Camaro, he chatted up the girls before he asked Regina out for tacos. The two began going out but Regina didn't like him...at first. Then she realized that he had some money and was all too willing to spend it on her.

"Oscar wasn't the typical guy that Regina would go for," Clark said. "Regina liked the 'bad boy', the thug. Oscar wasn't in street gang culture. He had immigrated from Mexico and actually had a real job, earning his living the old fashioned way as a truck driver. If anything, Regina would see someone like him as a sucker, someone who she could use."

Still, Regina was what Oscar wanted. He persisted in calling her, asking when he could see her again.

"He's a creepy guy," Regina told her sister, Margaret as her cell phone rang. She looked at the caller ID. Yep, it was Oscar.

"But maybe you can get some money from him?"

"Here, you talk to him," Regina said handing the cell phone to Margaret. "Just make up some baloney that I'm in jail or something."

"What?"

"Get rid of him. Tell him I need bail money."

"Hello, Oscar?" Margaret answered the phone.

"Yeah," Oscar said. "Who is this?"

"It's Margaret," she said, sounding as if she was trying to stifle tears. "Regina is in jail. She's locked up."

"What?"

"They put her in jail for something she didn't even do. They want one thousand dollars. One thousand dollars to bail her out."

Margaret smiled like a devil at her sister.

"I can help," Oscar said.

"No," Margaret said, sniffling. "It's too much."

"It's for your sister."

Oscar would persist in his willingness to help out, however. Margaret played him like a violin, agreeing to meet with Oscar to take his hard earned money.

"Oscar gave Margaret the money in the hopes of scoring points with the sisters," Clark said. "He thought that by being 'nice' and bailing them out of trouble they would find him attractive. Instead, it just fueled their contempt for him. These girls liked thugs. Bums. They cared little for Oscar's chivalry."

Regina would not use the money to pay back her mother, however. She would give the money to her real boyfriend, Johnny, who bought an "old school ride" car with Oscar's money.

Oscar would call Regina over twenty-four times during the next five days wanting to know what happened. He began to feel like the sucker he was.

He had a wife and kids in Mexico. But here in Chicago he fell for the brown-haired beauty and became all too willing to be her patsy.

"Oscar was playing with fire," Clark said. "He just didn't realize how far gone the girls were in terms of narcissism. He didn't see the fact that they didn't even see him as a human being. All he saw was batting eyelashes and pretty faces. He was totally smitten with Regina despite the fact that he had a wife and kids back in Mexico. Here he was, in Chicago, where he was free from the responsibilities of family. He could have a little fun and if he had to spend some money to do it, so be it."

CHAPTER THREE

The two sisters were surprised at how easy it was to extract money out of Oscar. With one fake phone call, they had one thousand dollars cash to their name.

"They were both attractive girls in the neighborhood," Clark said. "They were young, looking up to gang members and drug dealers for the power they had. But the girls realized that they had their own power. The power of budding sexuality that could make men do what they wanted. They could trick men into doing things for them with a future promise of sex."

Oscar continued to call and it would be only a matter of time before he would be confronted with the truth that he had been lied to. The girls had to construct a plan to get rid of him.

"I have an idea," Margaret said, picking up the cell phone and calling their fifteen year old friend, Veronica Garcia.

"Need your help," Margaret said as Veronica picked up.

"For what?" Veronica asked.

"I need a gun. Can you get a gun?"

"A gun?"

"Can your boyfriend get a gun?"

Veronica, like the DeFrancisco sisters, was enamored with street gang members. She had a boyfriend who could obtain whatever you needed, drugs or guns.

"Why?"

"We're going to stick up and rob Oscar," she said.

"You're not going to kill him are you?"

"We're just going to scare him a little," Margaret laughed.

Veronica did as she was asked, getting a gun from her boyfriend and heading straight over to the DeFrancisco sister's home.

"Nice," Margaret said, looking the pistol over, closing one eye as she looked through the cross hairs. "So where we going to do this?"

"Right here," Regina said, waving her hands around the living room.

"No way," Margaret said. "If the neighbors complain about us screaming and yelling then they're going to hear a gunshot. Duh."

Regina looked around the home. The basement door caught her eye.

"We'll lead him down there," Regina said, leading her sister down the basement steps. "Nobody can hear anything down here. The noise will be drowned out."

"Here," Margaret said, removing some blue tarp from the shelf. She spread the material down on the basement floor in front of the steps. "We can't leave any blood stains."

"Check you out," Regina laughed. "Miss Perry Mason."

Margaret laughed as she flattened out the tarp, placing it in a perfect line with the basement stairs. "Okay," she said, walking halfway up the steps. "So if we shoot him from here," pointing her forefinger into a gun. "He'll fall straight down there."

"Perfect."

The two sisters giggled and gave each other fist bump.

"Here is where the disconnect took place," Clark said. "They had embraced an environment and a culture where there were a lot of faux tough guys. Guys who said they would commit violence but for the most part it was all talk. The girls took it literally. At no point did they realize the gravity of what they were doing. They wanted to be 'gangstas', they wanted to be seen as 'hard'. They didn't have the maturity or the experience to realize that all of those 'gangstas' that they look up to are in jail. They didn't see Oscar at all. He was less than human. Something that is used, discarded and desecrated when it is no longer of use."

CHAPTER FOUR

Oscar was surprised that Regina finally called him back.

"Hey," she said, her teenaged voice soft and inviting.

"You're out of jail?" he asked.

"Yeah," she said. "I really appreciate what you did for me. That was really sweet of you."

"No worries," he said. "I need my money back. Been calling you like crazy."

"I'm sorry, I've just been busy."

"Yeah, I understand. But I need my money back."

"I was wondering if there was some other way I can pay you back?" she said in a sensual tone of voice.

"Like?"

"Like, I know you think my sister is hot, right?"

"What's that got to do with anything?"

"It is something we've been thinking about," she said. "But if you're not cool with it, it's okay."

"Not cool with what?"

"We were wondering if," Regina giggled. "If you can come over for a threesome."

Oscar couldn't believe his luck. He had heard of white girls being freaky, he just didn't think he would ever be able to experience it himself.

Naive to their plan, he rushed over and parked his car outside their mother's home in the South Side of Chicago.

He knocked on the door and was greeted by Margaret and Veronica Garcia, a friend of the two sisters. He didn't see the .38 caliber semi-automatic pistol had in her back waistband.

"Does anyone else know you're coming over?" Margaret asked.

"No," Oscar mumbled, shrugging his shoulder.

Margaret nodded her head and let the young man in. He saw Regina step into the room holding a bin of dirty laundry.

An awkward silence ensued followed by even more awkward smiles. The two sisters fed off each others willingness to go through with the plan. Even if one of them had second thoughts, they would be deemed "soft" by the other.

They had to go through with the murder.

Both women looked over at the young man with come hither looks. Regina said nothing as she opened the basement door and walked down.

"You go with Regina," Margaret said smiling.

"Right," Oscar said, his heart pounding in anticipation as he followed her down.

Oscar heard Margaret's footsteps behind him. What he didn't know was that she had a gun pointed at the back of his head.

When he reached the bottom step, she pulled the trigger.

The young man died instantly, falling face first in the tarp.

"Holy shit!" Margaret said. "I had no idea it would be that fucking loud. It doesn't sound that loud on TV."

Margaret came down the stairs. She kicked Oscar in the head hard, sending more blood spraying across the floor and wall.

"Nobody heard," Regina said as she knelt down and began rifling through Oscar's pockets.

"What the fuck was that?" Veronica said, calling down from the top of the basement steps.

"Did you see that? " Margaret asked. "He fell down like a baby!"

The sisters took out his wallet which had over $600 cash. They took his cell phone then ripped off the sterling silver chain from his neck.

"What the fuck happened?" Veronica said, her voice trembling as she came down a few steps.

"We shot his ass," Margaret said. "He's dead. Look at that shit, he's bleeding through his ears."

"Why did you do it?" Veronica screamed. "Why? Oh my God!"

"Shut the fuck up!" Margaret screamed.

"Don't just stand there," Regina commanded. "Come and help."

Their lifelong friend could only watch as the two sisters took out his car keys and wrapped up his body in a flowery bed sheet.

CHAPTER FIVE

"The girls suffered from what I call the 'Lord of the Flies' syndrome," Clark said. "Here they are hanging out with drug dealers, obtaining guns, killing men in the basement. There is no parental figure in sight! They are left to fend for themselves and the end result is murder and mayhem."

With the dead body in the basement, both sisters peeked out their window, waiting for dark.

Confident that the entire neighborhood was asleep, they opened the door and carried Oscar's body out of the home.

The three girls struggled carrying the dead weight, wrapping his body with a comforter and the flowered bed sheet.

They opened up the trunk and placed the body inside.

"What are you guys doing?" a woman yelled from a window across the street.

The girls looked up startled.

"We're getting rid of some furniture" Regina called out. "No worries."

The girls waved at the neighbor as she moved away from the window.

"Nosy bitch," Regina whispered.

Margaret giggled. Veronica still scared, said nothing.

They got into the vehicle and drove to a vacant lot where they took out Oscar's body again.

"This is hard work," Regina complained. "Shit!"

They plopped the body on the ground, looking at it for a beat before Regina reached back into the trunk. She pulled out a bottle of nail polish remover and poured the liquid over the tarp.

"Are you sure that's gonna work?" Margaret asked.

"It says 'highly flammable'," Regina said, shrugging her shoulders.

Margaret lit a match and set the material on fire.

The flame went up immediately, the girls could feel the warmth on their faces in the cold Chicago night.

"Told you this shit would work!" Regina said.

Then as fast as the flame started, it quickly died down.

"Light another one," Regina said.

Margaret threw down another match, getting the flames going again as Regina doused the tarp with the remaining nail polish remover.

Satisfied, the girls quickly got back into the Camaro and drove off.

**

An anonymous call came into police headquarters reporting the fire in the vacant lot. The caller investigated further, however, and saw Oscar's arm sticking out through the fire. He called 911 again with a sense of urgency, telling them of the body.

CHAPTER SIX

When police on scene identified Oscar Velazquez' partially burned body, their initial knee-jerk reaction was that this was the work of a local street gang, a drug deal gone awry. But when they found the nail polish remover bottle, however, they quickly realized that this was the work of amateurs. A jealous girlfriend maybe.

Meanwhile, the DeFrancisco sisters cruised around town over the following days, trying to pawn off the Camaro.

"This is where the sisters make the guys in 'Dumb and Dumber' look like geniuses," Clark said. "They had only pre-planned the front end of the murder. Like most impulsive killers, they had no idea what to do after. Their greed took over and they decide to sell the Camaro. They have no papers for it, duh, and really can only sell a stolen vehicle to a thug. They find no takers as even the dumbest street gang member isn't going to buy a hot car from two teenaged girls. So they cruise around town and Oscar's brother spots them in the car."

The girls, failing in their sales efforts, would later abandon he vehicle behind a storefront and set it on fire.

**

The day after Oscar's killing, a mutual friend named Jessica Benitez stopped by the house. Jessica went downstairs and watched Margaret mop up a stain of blood near the basement steps,

"The hell is that?" she asked.

Margaret said nothing as she poured bleach over the blood, scrubbing hard.

"Dude bled all over the floor," Regina said. "But only after Margaret kicked him in the head. We called him over, told this idiot we'd have a threesome with him. Then we robbed his ass."

"But the blood stain on the floor-" Jessica asked, watching Margaret clean up.

"We killed a guy," Margaret said without remorse.

"He was going to kill us!" Regina said. "Margaret shot him in the back of the head. We searched his body and found a gun in his waistband. Then we wrapped him up in plastic and put him in his car."

"Holy shit, girl," Jessica.

"We're about to go on the run," Margaret announced.

"Aren't you scared?" Jessica asked, looking back down at the blood stain in the basement.

"I ain't scared of nothing," Margaret said. "You should have seen his head when I shot him. His brain oozed out like cheese."

Margaret made a rolling motion with her hands.

Jessica then accompanied Margaret to the store she purchased a bottle of blonde hair dye for her "disguise."

"We see here how the whole street gang culture has influenced the behavior of these girls," Clark said. "At any point in time, Veronica or Jessica could have went straight to the police. But they get caught up in the drama of the moment. The so-called 'loyalty' to their friend who, quite frankly, would shoot them up in a heartbeat if they knew that they were going to be a snitch."

Going off the tip from Oscar's brother, the police show up to question both Regina and Margaret. The duo denied ever seeing Oscar.

They then go to interview Veronica Garcia.

They found the jittery fifteen year old to be a different story, however. The teen quickly crumbled under the pressure of questioning and told the police the entire story.

Feeling the heat, the DeFrancisco sisters go on the run...

CHAPTER SEVEN

For all of their stupidity in committing the murder, the DeFrancisco sisters deftly avoided capture for almost two years.

They decided to split up. Margaret would go to live with their maternal aunt in Roscoe, Illinois, an hour and a half drive away from where they lived. Roscoe was a small town with less then 10,000 people, a far cry from the drug infested streets of Chicago. Margaret's worst dreams were now realized. She was now a nerd who had to stay inside all day long, living in a boring cul-de-sac with no street gang action. Neighbors would remark that they would never see her and if hey did she would quickly go back inside.

Living underground without detection, it took a broadcast of the television show AMERICA'S MOST WANTED to generate an anonymous tip which led to Margaret's whereabouts. Police staked out her aunt's apartment and entered, finding Margaret in her bedroom with a blank look on her face.

"My feelings were hurt bad because she (my wife) did something behind my back," Margaret's uncle by marriage said later. "I knew (police) were going to find her anyway."

Seven months later, Regina was captured in Dallas living with her Latin King boyfriend, Johnny Rivera.

Initially, she did not even know where the gang banger lived. She just knew the town, Laredo, and she journeyed there by bus. Regina would eventually find him, locating one of his relatives. She would live under an alias and claimed that she worked as a maid.

Police knew better. Regina made money by selling drugs under the Latin King banner.

Unlike Margaret, Regina had evaded the scrutiny of the America's Most Wanted viewers.

Her capture came about because she could not stop hanging out with the wrong crowd.

Two sheriffs were had mistakenly arrived at her boyfriend's apartment, wanting to serve a warrant to someone else.

Rivera allowed the deputies to enter his apartment but he had left a marijuana flake on his table. Police searched the apartment further and found several packages of crack cocaine ready to be sold.

The deputies arrested Rivera. They searched inside the apartment and interviewed Regina, who was groggy from a cocaine high. She showed them her false Texas identification and they let her go.

But the deputies smelled something fishy on her aside from marijuana. They had the apartment manager set up a meeting with her. She arrived at the complex in an SUV with another man. The police approached and the SUV sped away.

The high-speed chase down residential Dallas streets reached upwards of 90 mph. The SUV then slammed into a center median, the front tires blowing out.

Regina got out of the car and tried to sprint away. A deputy tackled her and they fell to the ground, her cell phone skidding across the gravel road. Sifting through her pockets, the officer found over $1,500 cash.

She was taken to Dallas County Jail where they discovered her true identity.

"We pulled her out of jail," said a Deputy Dodson. "I asked to see one of her tattoos, and she showed me...I called her by name, but she never said a word to me. She knew it was over."

She was then extradited to Illinois to stand trial for the murder of Oscar Velazquez.

CHAPTER EIGHT

The trial of the two women began in July of 2004 and both sisters pleaded not guilty by reason of self-defense.

But their friend, Veronica Garcia, had cut a deal with prosecutors in return for a lesser sentence. She would provide the testimony that would damn the two sisters to prison.

Garcia said that she didn't know what the sisters had planned. She had simply provided the gun to the DeFrancisco's which she thought would be used for a robbery only.

"I didn't see her shoot Oscar," Veronica said.

The prosecution brought forth additional witnesses in Jessica Benitez, Luciana Macias, and Maria Constantino, the neighbor.

"Both of them told me that they killed Oscar," Jessica said. "Margaret kicked him in the head so he could die faster."

"I saw them load the body into the back of the Camaro," Constantino said. "Regina told me that she planned out the killing."

Margaret, however, maintained their innocence. She said that Oscar came to the apartment angry because the sisters had tricked him out of one-thousand dollars.

"I shot him to protect Regina," Margaret said.

"Then why didn't you tell the reporting officer what happened?" the prosecution attorney asked.

"We would've got in trouble," Margaret said. "If I told the truth, I would've been there longer."

Regina DeFrancisco would also take the stand and claim self-defense as well.

"I came out of my bedroom," Regina said. "And he was there, cursing and screaming. He pulled a gun on me. I thought I was going to die. I curled up on the floor, in a fetal position. I begged for my life. Then I heard a gunshot and saw Margaret standing over Oscar, holding a gun."

"Whose idea was it to dispose of the body?"

"Veronica knew of this vacant lot," Regina said. "It was her idea."

The jury would deliberate for over six and a half hours. Regina would be found guilty of murder. Margaret's jury, however, was unable to convict her. There was and 11 to 1 deadlock with one juror believing that she should be acquitted. The juror did not believe that someone so young could commit murder.

Margaret was then released from custody and told to await retrial. She had a baby during this time, a girl, and would find work as a nursing assistant while she awaited another trial.

Four months later, Margaret would be given another day in court. Veronica Garcia would once again be the star witness for the prosecution, detailing the exact same testimony as before.

There would be no deadlock in this second go around as Margaret would be convicted of first-degree murder.

Regina would be sentenced to 35 years in prison while Margaret would be sentenced to 46 years. Both women are now jailed at the Dwight Correctional Center. They have each filed appeals which have been denied.

"The girls cared nothing about Oscar Velazquez," Clark said. "In the end, they remained true to their own narcissistic nature. They only cared about what was happening to the next. They cared about nothing about the now fatherless children Oscar Velazquez would leave behind nor about the fact that the took his life."

Veronica Garcia was jailed for five years. She served her full sentence and has since been released.

"This is a cautionary tale if there ever was one," Clark said. "The sisters had it all. They had access to one of the finest schools in their state. Yet they chose to throw it all away for short money and the cheap thrill of the 'thug life.' In the end, they got to see what the 'thug life' was really all about. Mindless violence where everyone is out for themselves, especially when there is a plea bargain to be made. They could have had it all had they stayed on the straight and narrow. Now they have nothing."

WITCH KILLERS : THE TRUE STORY OF SUZAN AND MICHAEL CARSON

151

TAMMY BENNETT

"What started as two hippies going on an acid trip that quickly evolved into a serial killing couple. Suzan thought that she was giving a vision by Allah. She could go on to kill homosexuals and witches. The two then imagined themselves to be these heroic martyrs battling the forces of evil. They were nothing more than schizophrenic killers."

"Oh God!"

"Sir, what is the address?" the police dispatcher asked for the second time.

"She's dead. There's blood everywhere. Everywhere."

The panicked landlord had just discovered the body of his tenant in her basement apartment in San Francisco. She was lying face down in a pool of blood, covered by a blanket.

Her name was Keryn Barnes. Twenty-three years old with long blonde hair and wholesome features that looked like someone you would meet at a church social.

The landlord had enlisted the aid of a plumber to go investigate the basement apartment he owned on Schrader Street in San Francisco. He had not heard or seen the lovely young woman that he had rented the place out to and was worried about her.

His worst fears would soon become realized.

Police would find no signs of forced entry and Keryn still had money in her purse. She did not appear to have been raped.

Keryn had sustained several blows to the head which caused a skull fracture. The coroner found a bloodied iron skillet in the kitchen cabinet and upon further examination determined that the young woman suffered twelve to thirteen stab wounds to the neck and face.

The apartment wall was painted with mysterious religious symbols, spiral shaped ankhs, triangles and other arcane drawings.

On the bottom of one wall, however, netted one clue.

The name "Suzan" was scrawled in black ink.

Police would go on to interview some of Keryn Barnes' friends and they would find out that the young woman had taken in a strange couple by the name of Michael and Suzan Bear. Keryn had met the two hippies at a party in the Haight-Ashbury district, becoming immediate friends.

"I know something about you," Suzanne said to the young Keryn. "You're anxious. You're curious. I know because I used to be like you. You know, searching. But Michael and I we got something, man. All you have to do is sit still. Sit still and let the power of the universe flow inside you."

Keryn listened in rapt attention as the older woman passed the joint to her.

"That's right," Michael said, eyeballing the blonde beauty in front of him. She was younger than Suzan but he could not bring himself to lust after another woman. Or could he? "This culture we live in, our minds and bodies have become disconnected. There's a whole conspiracy to set minds apart from our true selves. Mind and body have to be one. We have to fight against all of the evil forces that prevent that from happening."

Barnes loved the counterculture of the San Francisco scene and felt a kinship with the weird couple. These were the kind of people she wanted to meet, so different from the people she grew up in Georgia. They had their own belief systems and were not constrained by polite society.

In her eyes, they were "cool."

The Bears would talk to Keryn about transcendental meditation, psychic phenomena and their own interpretation of the Muslim religion in which the young woman found fascinating. The two hippies needed a place "to crash for a little while" and Keryn took pity on the duo, allowing them to stay with her.

She slowly became drawn into their way of thinking, becoming their acolyte but having no idea how dangerous they really were.

The Bears had no criminal record but they were about to embark on a murder spree in which they would avoid capture for over two years.

And Keryn Barnes would be their first victim.

SUZAN CARSON

On the surface, Suzanne Carson lived an otherwise normal life growing up in Arizona in the 1950s. Her father was a newspaper executive while her mother was a housewife. As she grew older, however, she became more reclusive. She truly believed she was psychic and because of her introverted nature she had very few friends. Suzanne did very poorly in school, suffering from severe dyslexia.

Suzanne would marry, becoming a housewife just like her own mother. She lived in Scottsdale but she did not put on the false front of being happily married. She had a teenage son and often flirted with his friends.

She had the life of privilege, her husband was wealthy and she would spend her afternoons playing tennis. In the end, however, Suzanne was accustomed to the wealth from both her upbringing and now her marriage. She wanted something more. She wanted power, authority and attention.

A sexual predator, she played the role of "Mrs.Robinson" to her son's high school classmates, shamelessly flirting and going out on "dates" with them. In later interviews, she would brag that she bedded "over one-hundred fifty" of her son's classmates. These sexual rendezvous were intensified with her use of hallucinogenic drugs (acid, peyote, hash, marijuana).

Suzanne went on an acid trip with one of her son's high school friends then woke up in the morning to find her entire living room painted in red triangles with the name "Suzan" written at the bottom. Not remembering what she did the previous evening, Suzanne claimed that there was "a hole in my head" and that "all of the electricity in the house" was now flowing through her.

Suffering from these delusions, Suzanne would describe her own visual hallucinations.

"Suzanne was a schizophrenic," forensic psychologist Paula Flowers said. "It grew worse as she got older and she obviously needed psychiatric assistance. She needed to have been diagnosed, medicated and perhaps even institutionalized. But this was the early 1980s and we didn't have a lot of the mental health precautions in place like we have now. She was, in essence, a functional schizophrenic. The people she came in contact with would write off her strange ramblings as coming from someone who was a 'bit off'. And when she moved to San Francisco she fit right in."

"We can argue that Suzanne may have been medicating herself with the daily use of drugs," Flowers said. "Her use of hallucinogenic drugs increased as the years went on. She would have 'visions' as she would call them but a doctor would call them delusions and consider her to be very, very dangerous. When you combine acid tripping with schizophrenia you can get a lethal cocktail and that is what we got with Suzan. The drugs would only enhance her bizarre visions and make things much worse."

Suzan grew tired of the role as a housewife while her husband grew tired of her bizarre thought processes and behavior. Her husband would divorce her and take his two children with him. She was now free to embrace the counterculture and free love philosophy that she always wanted.

She began developing her own radical interpretation of the Islamic religion and with her new found identity she changed her name from Suzanne to Suzan, thinking that the mess she created in the living room was some kind of sign from Allah.

Suzan took bits and pieces from the Islamic religion to fit her own needs as she enjoyed mescaline and marijuana. Square jawed and wild eyed, Suzan began losing her physical attractiveness and noticed that the teenage boys no longer paid too much attention to her.

She needed a new man.

Around the age of 35, she went through a serious acid trip and began to have visions. These visions called for her to have a spiritual partner to "complete her destiny".

She would meet this man in James Carson.

JAMES CARSON

James Carson was born in 1950 in Oklahoma. He grew up in a normal middle class family. His father was an oil engineer while his mother was a schoolteacher.

His childhood was typical until he was diagnosed with a rare bone disorder when he was very young. He was put on bed rest for several years where he devoured books of philosophy, religion, politics and history.

He grew to have a combative personality, however, regularly using drugs and alcohol.

"Part of James' mental illness was that he thought everyone was about to get him," Flowers said. "There would be no way in hell he could hold down a job. He was anti-social and argumentative, willing to take offense at the most minor details."

James would take a stab at normalcy, however, as he would meet a woman named Lynn at the University of Iowa where he obtained a masters degree in Chinese studies. The couple married, had a child, then moved to Arizona.

His wife worked while James stayed at home to take care of his young daughter. He was a loving father but his anti-social tendencies ran deep. He hated the government, believed in conspiracies and soon became impossible to live with. Lynn divorced James and soon afterward he met Suzan.

Long-haired and bearded, James cut a Charles Manson-esque appearance. His eyes were empty and soulless, often greeting people with an expressionless glare.

CRAZY AND CRAZIER

When the two first met at a party, there was instant chemistry. Suzan was nine years older, taking on the mother/God role that James seemed to be looking for. He loved Buddhist philosophy and had been waiting his whole life for a woman like Suzan, someone who turned her back on mainstream American values. Suzan liked younger men, she liked being looked upon as a mother figure, a spiritual guide that led young men into drug-crazed nights where she was the center of their world.

Suzan was looking for someone to worship her and she found that in James who made her feel sexually attractive again.

"They both described their meeting as instant electric attraction," Jenn Carson said, the daughter of James. "From that very moment that they met, they were just joined like magnets."

"Me and you," Suzan said meeting James for the first time. "We're the same."

"That right?"

"There is a defiance in you. You are who you are and you are going to stick to your guns. We're the same, you and I. There is a whole world out there that is trying to suffocate who we are. We can fight back. We can take our swords into battle together."

Suzan saw James as a reflection of who she was and the two begin a daily routine of pot, alcohol and hallucinogenic drugs. They would have daily discussions on the problems of the world and how only they understood it.

James, in essence, becomes Suzan's follower in their cult of two. They both had the same spiritual fantasies and they both suffered from mental illness.

Baptizing James into her self-made religion, Suzan decided that he should change his name. She christened him as "Michael", in reference to the archangel from the Bible who fought demons. They adopt the last name of "Bear" as James may have used his childhood fascination with the animals as inspiration.

"What we see happening is a reinvention of themselves," Flowers said. "By taking on these new identities they shed all of the ghosts of their past. Renaming themselves was a symbolic gesture, their way of taking control and being rid of the societal forces that they felt were keeping them down. They were free to recreate a new person and that person would have power. That person would be special, given a license from God himself to go and rid the world of evil."

The couple would go on acid trips and engage in their own invented prayer sessions. They would talk in tongues, read from selected verses in the Koran and then indulge in yoga-inspired chants. Michael was well-versed in eastern religions but again followed Suzan's lead as she went from one discipline to another in her mescaline-fueled prayer sessions.

"My father had always been interested in very radical religious beliefs," Jenn Carson said. "Those interests became more and more extreme."

"It was the most bizarre environment you can imagine. It was like being dropped into a rabbit hole. You have two individuals who both have mental health needs and now they're using very, very heavy drugs."

Suzanne would have visions, seeing kaleidoscopic lights through trees, strange elephant like creatures and ancient bronze statues with no form.

"Suzan truly believed that she was going crazy," Flowers said. "She had to recognize that her own brain was not functioning properly so perhaps that is why she believed that there was a divine entity that was telling her to commit these acts. She thought everyone was out to get them. The FBI was out to get them. A secret government agency was out to get them. Yet Allah is the force that is on their side."

Michael convinced her, however, that her delusions were a gift. Like an old time Biblical prophet, Suzanne was chosen to receive these visions from Allah.

"You're a prophet," Michael said with excitement. "You're a yogi. You're not a witch. You have been given privileged access. Your visions are a gift!"

"Maybe you're right," Suzan rubbed her head.

"There's a reason why Allah is invisible. Have you ever thought about that? No one else can see him. But you can hear him."

"There's a war coming," Suzan said. "God will send someone to fight the Evil. And that someone is us. That's what he's saying to me."

"That's right."

"Everyone will die," Suzan said, lowering her voice just in case someone from the government was listening. "Everyone who practices witchcraft. Homosexuals. Witches. All of the evil people. We have to look beyond ourselves. The police. The government. Celebrities and politicians. Every bad person will burn in fire!"

The vision fit in line with Michael's own paranoid schizophrenic personality. He saw witches everywhere, the government, the media, the person on the street.

Deluded and convinced of their own righteousness, they became a "cult" of two.

The duo would move to California for a new life, settling into the Haight-Ashbury district.

"They were on the hunt for new recruits," Flowers said. "I don't think they had clarity as to the type of person they were going for, male or female. They were simply looking for someone young and open-minded."

They would meet Keryn Barnes at the party and she would take the couple in.

"She (Keryn) was kind of interested in that eclectic scene," Jenn Carson said. "And she was very much a bohemian girl. When Suzan and Michael entered her life I think she found them fascinating."

"Keryn was young and impressionable," Flowers said. "She had embraced that whole San Francisco counterculture mentality where you do not judge anyone. She probably didn't see herself as a follower in their cult. She wanted some older people to hang out with, people who were different from her. She could not see what anyone in their right mind could see in Suzan and Michael. They were weird, crazy and dangerous."

Suzan, however, would grow jealous of the beauty of Keryn. She would notice the sideways glances that Michael would give the pretty and young Keryn.

"Suzan would look in the mirror and see an old lady with yellow teeth," Flowers said. "She wore no make-up and she had thick jawline with deepening wrinkles. She compared herself to the young Keryn and felt inferior."

Fearing that she would lose Michael, she began brainwashing her younger lover into believing that Keryn was a witch.

"Do you think she's pretty?" Suzan asked as Michael watch Keryn head into the bathroom.

"Yeah," he said, nodding his head without commitment.

"Keryn's a witch," Suzan said.

"No," Michael said. "Keryn is cool, man."

"She's siphoning away my youth," Suzan said. "Taking away my powers as a yogi. She's trying to come between us. I can feel it. She's doing it psychically. I know she is."

"What?"

"She's a witch. She must be dealt with."

"No."

"We have to kill the witch," Suzan said, looking deep her lover's eyes. "Michael, you have to kill Keryn."

"Suzan truly believed she had psychic powers," Flowers said. "She would look Michael directly in his eyes and try and communicate to him through telepathy. She thought she had ESP. He would always comply so his obedience would only provide further evidence that she did have psychic powers."

Repressing his growing lust for Keryn like any good religious disciple, Michael would obey his mother figure in Suzan.

On March 7th, 1981, Michael Bear Carson would kill Keryn Barnes, attacking her with a frying skillet as she slept on the floor.

He fractured her skill before stabbing her with a paring knife.

"Suzan and Michael portrayed Keryn as a witch," Jenn Carson said. "As a woman who was trying to break up a marriage. None of those things were true. This was a nice girl from Georgia. No one should go through what she went through. She was beautiful, delightful twenty-three year old girl."

"All of the crazy and deluded talk they have done has now come to a head," Flowers said. "They've just killed their first 'witch'. They both have delusions of grandeur in ridding the world of more 'witches', so away they go to kill as many 'witches' as they can."

Suzan and Michael then went on the run, heading toward Oregon.

They would find an isolated cabin in the woods and enjoy what they would call their own "private paradise". The anti-social couple were away from people and frolicked in the wilderness.

"This was meant to be," Suzan said, twirling around underneath the tall Oregon trees. "This is our reward for being good servants to Allah."

"This is true wealth," Michael said looking across the Oregon landscape, smelling the scent of the jasmine flowers. "Not something that you buy. It is contentment of the soul."

"We can stay here forever," she said. "But let us not forget that we are 'hash-ashins'. Islamic assassins. We must go out and search for more prey. There is still plenty of evil in the world. But this will be our refuge. Our safe-house."

Their delusions were short-lived, however, as the couple soon ran out of food and supplies in the cabin. Michael would hitch-hike into the nearest town where he met a local construction worker who let the couple stay in his tree house.

The man soon felt uncomfortable with the arrangement as Suzan said very little. She would laugh and smile at inappropriate moments.

Suzan had a way of looking at a person, she would stare and then smile as if she knew something that the person didn't.

She gave him the creeps.

Sensing that the couple was dangerous, the man sent a thug armed with a gun to kick the couple out as they headed back to California.

They would find a marijuana plantation in California and land a job of care taking the illegal operation in a remote part of Humboldt County.

The couple did not make friends with anyone at the plantation and soon locked horns with a man named Clark Stevens who was part owner. Stevens could be gruff, not averse to four letter words and looked down on hired help hippies like Michael and Suzan.

Michael had an assigned post working security, standing guard at the fence in front of the hidden plantation. Stevens pulled up, honked his horn and demanded to be let into the farm.

"No one is supposed to be here today," Michael said, blocking the front gate as Stevens came out of his jeep.

"That right?" Stevens said. "Who the hell are you?"

"Who the hell are you?" Michael challenged back.

"I own this fucking place!" Stevens said. "Open the fucking gate."

"No," Suzan said. "Michael, you know you can't let him through. It is your job."

"Tell your bitch to shut up and open the fucking gate!" Stevens grew more agitated.

Suzan would see Stevens as a man that needed to be eliminated. Stevens would later criticize the way the hippie couple handled the plants and wanted them out off the plantation. The couple, however, decided to nip the flower in the bud and take care of Stevens themselves.

"He disrespected me," she said to Michael.

"What do you want me to do?"

"He touched me!" Suzan said, the words hissing from her mouth. "Are you going to let him get away with that?"

Suzan detailed a story in which she believed that Stevens had made a sexual pass at her. This gave Michael carte blanche to commit his murder.

Michael then confronted Stevens inside the plantation grounds and shot him in the head.

"Michael shot Stevens on the orders of Suzan," Flowers said. "She thought that Stevens had disrespected her and used Michael as her weapon of choice. That was part of her mental make-up, to use Michael as her hit man, so to speak. If she saw that someone needed eliminating she would snap her fingers and Michael would do her bidding. Disrespecting Suzan would be met with a death sentence."

The two then chopped up Stevens body, doused his body with kerosene and set him on fire.

"Just looking at the level of brutality," Flowers said. "The Stevens murder was a step beyond the Barnes murder with the added desecration of a dismemberment and burning of the corpse. The 'Witch Killers' weren't the type of serial murderers that had a set modus operandi. They were opportunistic and random which is what made them so hard to catch."

Police would later discover Stevens' body by accident when a helicopter spotted one of the dogs playing with what at first glance seemed like a ball.

Looking closer, they realized that the dog was playing with a human head.

The investigating police would later smell the body of Stevens before they saw it. His body had been only partially burned as the couple had covered him up with chicken manure which had been used to fertilize the marijuana plants.

KILLING RONALD REAGAN

The couple began making out a hit list of prominent figures they wanted to kill. At the top of the list stood Ronald Reagan and Johnny Carson.

The couple believed that the first, middle and last names had six letters. They saw supernatural significance in the numbers 666, the designation of the beast.

Still on the run, the couple would drive toward a roadblock. Police had blockaded the road looking for another criminal but the couple had mistakenly believed that the investigation was for them.

They stopped their stolen vehicle and immediately ran into the northern California woods. Deputies gave chase and would see Michael drop his backpack.

Inside his belongings, they would find his book which he titled "Cry For War."

"The book contained passages of Michael's philosophical beliefs," Flowers said. "Rambling on and on, it did attract interest of both the FBI and Secret Service, however, because the book wrote of assassinating the President. So now the deluded couple who imagined that big, black government helicopters were out to get them had to now face the real thing."

CAUGHT BY ACCIDENT

Michael would later be detained by police as he fit the description of a rapist. He had stolen some identification from someone else and gave the police that false information.

The police took his picture and faxed it over to the hospital so the rape victim could make a positive identification.

The victim said hat it wasn't him and Michael was released.

Taking to the road again, the couple began hitch-hiking. They were soon picked up by a man named John Hillyer.

"The couple now had more than a little blood lust in them," Flowers said. "They no longer limited themselves to killing people that they perceived as 'witches'. Now anyone that showed them the slightest amount of disrespect would be in mortal danger."

"You folks need a lift?" Hillyer called out.

Michael gave a thumbs up to the driver, moving toward the vehicle until Suzan stopped him. "He might be a witch," she said. "We're going to have to kill him."

The couple climbed into Hillyer's pick up truck. Suzan sat in between the two men. Hillyer played country music on the radio which Suzan hated.

"Witch music," she whispered.

Then Hillyer's leg accidentally brushed against hers.

Suzan interpreted the touch as a sexual pass. She looked at Michael, gazing deep into his eyes. Without saying a word, she tried to communicate to him through telepathy that he had to kill Hillyer.

Michael said nothing as he took out his gun.

"Hey man," Hillyer said. "What the hell is that?"

Michael hesitated. Then he pointed the gun at Hillyer.

Hillyer grabbed the gun and a struggle ensued. Suzan got into the middle of the fracas, scratching and clawing at the driver.

"The fuck is wrong with you people!" Hillyer screamed.

The fight for the gun continued for ten minutes, Hillyer trying to wrest the weapon away from Michael while Suzan screamed and bit him.

The car skidded to a stop on the highway.

Hillyer stepped out of vehicle, letting go of the gun.

There were witnesses. Surely, this crazed couple would not shoot him in broad daylight with all these people around who could identify them.

Hillyer attempted to sprint over to the side of the road.

"John jumped out to run for his life," Jenn Carson said. "And Suzan and Michael proceeded to both stab and shoot him on the side of the road in full view of commuters driving by. John died on the side of the road."

"John died because Suzan ordered it," Flowers said. "Michael was the willing patsy, a violent enabler, if you will. He did all these things to make her happy. Hillyer had innocently brushed his leg up against Suzan's. In Suzan's demented world, that was a capital offense."

The numerous witnesses, however, allowed the police to positively identify and capture the killers, ending their rampage.

MEDIA COVERAGE

In a bizarre twist, the couple held their own public news conference where they were allowed to detail their deluded philosophy. The two then went on a five-hour televised rant in which they justified their killings as a war on witchcraft.

"We rid the world of evil!" Suzan proclaimed. "Witches. People with dark forces."

"They did talk about the murders," Jenn Carson said. "And laid down this case that they were being spiritually attacked and that they had to defend themselves. That they were called to kill witches, their whole rationale."

The press conference was broadcast by KGO-TV in the San Francisco Bay Area.

"Their delusions were made public," Flowers said. "In hindsight, this really set a wrong precedent as it gave two deluded people a public stage. A part of me thinks that a defense attorney staged this in order to make the case that these two should not be able to competent to stand trial. If that was the case, it didn't work thankfully."

"In looking back, we see these two mentally ill people who were totally convinced in their psychotic beliefs. In their delusions of grandeur, they wanted the world to know of their work."

On June 4th, 1984, Suzan and Michael Carson were found guilty of the first degree murder of Keryn Barnes. Later, they were found guilty of the murders of Clark Stevens and John Hillyer.

Both were sentenced to a total of 75 years to life.

"Michael and Suzan were like dynamite and a match," Jenn Carson said. "Without the other, would this have occurred? I don't know."

Jenn Carson has now come to terms with her father being a serial killer.

"I would describe my father as brilliant," Jenn Carson recalled. "Handsome. Charming. Damaged. Misguided and soulless."

"I think Suzan is intelligent," Jenn Carson said. "And crazy. And evil."

"You absolutely cannot have rehabilitation when there is absolutely no remorse," Carson said. "Neither of these people feel any remorse whatsoever. They speak about it, in a way that almost glamorizes it, and Suzan has bragged about being friends with the Manson girls in prison. There doesn't seem to be any sign whatsoever that they would come out changed in any way."

James Carson is incarcerated at Mule Creek State Prison while Suzan is jailed at the Central California Women's Facility.

They were both up for parole in 2015, becoming eligible because of their age and prison overcrowding.

Both were denied.